HAWAII'S TOURISM LIFE CYCLE

PAST | PRESENT | UNCERTAIN FUTURE

DEXTER J. L. CHOY, PH.D.
PROFESSOR EMERITUS

SHIDLER COLLEGE OF BUSINESS
SCHOOL OF TRAVEL INDUSTRY MANAGEMENT
UNIVERSITY OF HAWAII AT MANOA

Hawaii's Tourism Life Cycle

Past | Present | Uncertain Future

Published by Dexter J.L. Choy, Ph.D.

Cover and Title Page by Greg Chinn

eBook ISBN: 978-1-7378075-0-6
Print ISBN: 978-1-7378075-1-3

THIS BOOK IS AFFECTIONATELY DEDICATED

TO MY WIFE

FOR HER LOVE AND SUPPORT THROUGHOUT

THE YEARS

Acknowledgements

I developed the outline for this book over twenty years ago but never had the large blocks of time necessary to complete the research and writing. This book would not have been possible without the support of my wife in taking on additional work and responsibilities to allow me the time to work on the book every day without any interruptions for a year. I wanted the book to be easily understood by non-specialists. My wife, a retired elementary teacher, was the first to read the manuscript. She provided editing and criticism to improve the readability of the book.

I would like to express my sincere thanks to David Flynn for his assistance throughout the years in using the University of Hawaii Library system to search for published materials related to travel and tourism. I also must thank Brian Richards, who saved me countless hours by guiding me on how to use Zotero to collect, organize and cite the references used in the book.

Special thanks go to Greg Chinn for designing the book cover and title page. The design of the book cover reflects a modern academic approach using the University of Hawaii Manoa colors–green, black, silver, and white. The interlocking circles represent the connections between the past, present and uncertain future. The Hawaiian Islands colored in green symbolizes harmony with nature and the environment.

Many thanks to Ann Miller for her generous gift of time and expertise in doing the final editing of the book. Thanks also to Paul Brewbaker for sharing his expert knowledge of the Hawaiian economy and allowing me to use his analysis in the book. Finally, I would like to thank Clara Hur, Kate Igoe, Keau George and Daniel Feher for their assistance in using the pictures and maps in the book.

List of Contributors in Alphabetical Order

- Greg Chinn, Creative Director, Local Brand Company
- Lucille Choy, retired
- Paul Brewbaker, economist, and principal, TZ Economics
- Daniel Feher, owner, and certified cartographer, FreeWorld Maps.net
- David Flynn, Business & Social Sciences Librarian, University of Hawaii at Manoa
- Keau George, Collections Manager, Hula Preservation Society
- Clara Hur, Library Technician, Hawaii State Archives
- Kate Igoe, Rights Management Archivist, Archive Division, National Air & Space Museum
- Ann Miller, Freelance Writer
- Colleen Okada, IT Specialist, School of Travel Industry Management, University of Hawaii at Manoa
- Brian Richards, Instructional Design Librarian, University of Hawaii at Manoa

Preface

The inspiration for writing this book comes from researching and teaching courses on tourism for over forty years as a professor at the School of Travel Industry Management, University of Hawaii at Manoa. Among several courses that I taught, my favorite course was Tourism Development in Hawaii and the Asia-Pacific Region. This book reflects the research which I developed for the course and for articles published in academic journals. Hawaii's success as a tourist destination always has been of interest to professionals and academics throughout the world. This is the first book that covers the historical development of tourism in Hawaii from the late 1780s to 2019. It offers a different perspective of the key factors that contributed to Hawaii's success. My experience as a consultant and lecturer throughout the Asia-Pacific region provided valuable knowledge and insights on underlying factors that influence tourism growth.

The conclusions of the book raise questions about past actions in Hawaii that have not been successful, and options are offered on how to move forward in the face of an uncertain future. It is hoped the book will begin a discussion on what should be done to ensure that tourism contributes to the welfare and benefit of residents as the primary objective. The pause in tourism caused by the Covid-19 pandemic has created an opportunity for a new beginning for the future of tourism in Hawaii.

Any errors in the book are my sole responsibility.

Table of Contents

Chapter 1

Introduction

Overview

Hawaii is the most isolated island chain in the world. As can be seen in the map of countries and islands in the Pacific region, Hawaii is located near the middle of the Pacific Ocean. Honolulu is located 2,392 miles (3,850 kilometers) west of San Francisco, 4039 miles (6,500 kilometers) east of Tokyo, and 4,536 miles (7,300 kilometers) northeast of Australia. Given its remoteness, it is amazing that Hawaii became one of the most well-known tourist destinations in the world. Hawaii often has been referred to as the Crossroads of the Pacific. Historically, ships and airplanes stopped off in Hawaii to resupply and refuel.

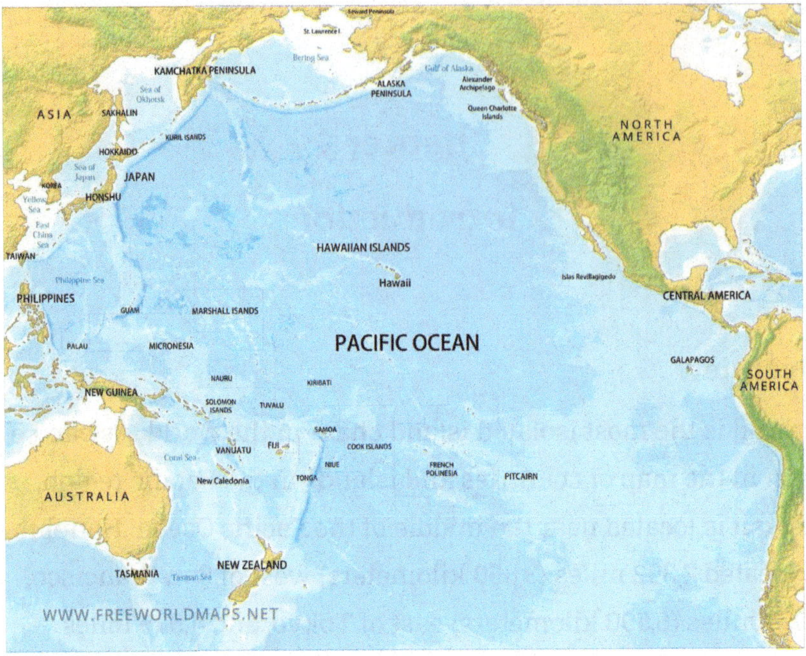

Figure 1.1: Countries and islands of the Pacific region
Source: Courtesy of FreeWorldMaps.net (https://www.freeworldmaps.net/ocean/pacific/pacific-countries-map.jpg)

This geographical advantage as a crossroads has been lost in modern days with the advent of long-haul aircraft and other forms of technology, which make it possible to bypass Hawaii for most commercial activities. Hawaii, nevertheless, has maintained its dominance as the most popular tourist destination in the Pacific islands.

Data on visitor arrivals to Hawaii are available as far back as 1927. One of the earliest technical studies on Hawaii's tourism was *Tourist Expenditures in the Territory of Hawaii* by Merton Cameron published in 1933 (Cameron 1933). This has been followed by numerous studies on tourist expenditures and their impacts throughout the years. Visitor arrivals, visitor characteristics and expenditure data now are collected on an annual basis by the State of Hawaii Department of Business, Economic Development & Tourism (DBET). In addition, visitor satisfaction surveys and surveys of resident attitudes toward tourism have been done periodically.

During the 1950s, there was high interest in Hawaii's tourism as it was looked upon to develop the economy after the war years. A report on the tourist industry of Hawaii was completed by John Child and Co. in 1951. Research reports of the Hawaii Visitors Bureau (HVB) were being published in the 1950s. In these early years, the government also was interested in developing the tourist industry in Hawaii as evidenced by a report on the role of government in developing Hawaii's visitor industry, and studies on Waikiki and the Neighbor Islands as potential tourist destinations. In 1959, the Hawaii State Planning Office was directed to undertake a study on Visitor Destination Areas in Hawaii (Hawaii. State Planning Office 1960). The study was completed in 1960 and provided a blueprint for tourism development in the islands.

The Hawaii State Planning Office, Economic Research Center of the University of Hawaii, as well as independent researchers, continued to analyze specific aspects of Hawaii's tourism during the 1960s to increase their understanding of the industry and identify opportunities for businesses to develop. Statistical modeling of the industry was done by researchers to measure economic impacts. Studies on potential markets from which to attract visitors to Hawaii and visitor satisfaction surveys were being done to identify how Hawaii could improve its desirability as a tourist destination. In later years, the question of success spoiling Waikiki was considered and whether there would be an adequate labor force for the industry. Private companies were becoming actively involved with developing the industry as evidenced by land development plans for converting agricultural lands to tourism uses. Most of these early development plans were proprietary and not published.

The 1970s was a decade of government planning for developing tourism. Goals for Hawaii's visitor industry were recommended by the first Travel Industry Congress held in Honolulu during January 1970 (Hawaii Visitors Bureau 1970). The main issues involved economic development and tourism impacts. A critical question was whether benefits from tourism exceeded costs related to tourism. A cost-benefit analysis was done by Mathematica Inc. for the Department of Planning and Economic Development (DPED), which later became the Department of Business Economic Development & Tourism (DBEDT) (Mathematica 1970). The study concluded that tax revenues from tourism exceeded the cost of public services related to tourism. A State Tourism Study was published in 1978 followed by a State Tourism Plan and Functional Plans for development of the industry (Hawaii. Office of Tourism 1978). The cost-benefit study did not deal with the social impacts of tourism. Independent researchers such as Finney and Watson raised questions about the negative impacts of tourism (Finney and Watson 1975).

Although the focus of tourism studies during the 1980s remained focused on the development and marketing of the industry, researchers were beginning to analyze qualitative aspects of the industry. The first major book on Hawaii's tourism was *Hawaii: The Legend That Sells* by Brian H. Farrell published in 1982 (Farrell 1982). Farrell was a professor of geography at the

University of California, Santa Cruz (UCSC). He was brought to UCSC to start a Center for South Pacific Studies and served as its director. He also served as the chair for the Environmental Studies Department. Part of the research and writing of the book was done when he was in Hawaii as a Visiting Professor at the School of Travel Industry Management (TIM), University of Hawaii. While at the School of TIM, he taught a course on social aspects of tourism which reflected his interest in the socio-economic and environmental impacts of tourism. As a non-resident, Farrell provided an external view of the conflicts between residents and western values, interest groups, politics, and the bureaucracy. His book was followed by studies on resident attitudes toward tourism and environmental impacts of tourism. A Strategic Plan for tourism was published in 1988 (Hawaii Department of Planning and Economic Development 1988).

Another seminal book, *Islands in Transition: The Past, Present, and Future of Hawaii's Economy* by Thomas Kemper Hitch was published in 1992 (T. K. Hitch 1992). Hitch provides an insider's view of the issues facing the islands from his long career in Honolulu's business community, first as Director of Research for the Hawaii Employers Council from 1950-1959 and then as Senior Vice President for Research at First Hawaiian Bank from 1959-1982. In 1958, Hitch's article, "Hawaii-Island Paradise with Economic Potential" was published in *Business Horizons* (T. Hitch 1958). His personal experience and knowledge of the islands extended from pre-Statehood to his passing in 1989. Hitch analyzed why Hawaii has enjoyed the highest standards of living in Oceania as well as provided answers to questions on the impact of foreign investment, low paying jobs, and prospects for the major sectors of Hawaii's economy, with tourism being the largest private sector of the economy.

Concerns over tourism's growth and its impact on the social, cultural, and environmental aspects of Hawaii increased during the 1990s. A Congress on Coastal and Marine Tourism was held in 1990 to see how conservation and economic development could be balanced (Miller and Auyong 1991). Government reports and other studies focused on issues such as the carrying capacity of tourism, preservation of cultural values and diversification of Hawaii's economy. A Tourism Congress was held in 1993, followed by a Tourism Mini-Congress in 1994. Studies on positioning Hawaii as an eco-tourism destination, promotion of sports and developing health-related tourism were completed by 1995. The 1990s was a period of no growth in visitor arrivals, and there were concerns over the competitiveness of Hawaii. In response to the difficulties faced by the tourism industry, the Hawaii Tourism Authority (HTA) was created in 1998 through a legislative act to serve as the State's lead agency supporting tourism.

The 21st century began with events that negatively affected Hawaii's tourism as well as travel in general. The first major event was the crash of the technology sector of the U.S. economy resulting in a stock market crisis beginning in May 2000. This was followed by the devastating bombing of the World Trade Center on September 11, 2001. Essentially no growth in visitor arrivals was experienced from 2000-2004. The HTA published the Hawaii Tourism Strategic Plan in 2005 to guide the growth of the industry from 2005-2015 (Hawaii Tourism Authority 2005). The goal was to move toward achieving a sustainable tourism industry from an economic, social, and environmental basis. How to minimize the negative effects of tourism upon society and the environment has proven to be elusive for most major tourist destinations.

The discussion, thus far, does not include numerous articles written in the media, academic journals, business, and other publications. Media articles, business and other publications tend to report current events which can add descriptive details to the analysis of Hawaii's tourism. Academic journals typically publish theoretical and empirical research which will be drawn upon in discussing the conceptual framework for analyzing tourism. Persons outside of the industry usually only see travel and tourism from a consumer's perspective. The tourism industry involves multiple segments of the economy in transporting people from their homes to their destinations and providing a satisfying experience at the destination. Business practices and strategies have evolved through the years to meet ever increasing demands from travelers.

Objectives of the Book

There have been numerous studies on Hawaii's tourism, but most published studies have been government funded or technical studies analyzing specific aspects of tourism. The business aspects of tourism typically have not been analyzed in previous studies of Hawaii's tourism. This book examines how Hawaii developed and grew into one of the most popular tourist destinations in the world. The analysis is provided from three perspectives: 1) a conceptual framework for analyzing tourism; 2) historical development of tourism with attention to key factors which influenced the growth of tourism, underlying patterns of development, and business strategies; and 3) Hawaii's experience within the context of world travel, especially the Asia-Pacific region.

Information Sources

Information for this book was drawn from a variety of sources including published reports, books, and academic journal articles. The key sources for information on tourism in Hawaii prior to World War II were Anson Chong, *Economic Development of Hawaii, and the Growth of Tourism before 1945*; L.J. Crampon, *An Inquiry into the Development of Tourism in Hawaii 1770 to 1970*; and R.S. Kuykendall & A.G. Day, *Hawaii—A History from Polynesian Kingdom to American Statehood* (Chong 1963; Crampon 1973; Kuykendall 1961).

Information on tourists is drawn from data bases of the United Nations World Tourism Organization (UNWTO), HVB, HTA, DBEDT, and individual countries. A conceptual framework for analyzing the tourism industry uses the UNWTO definitions of travelers and tourists; the U.S. Department of Commerce definition of trips; and concepts from The Travel Industry by Gee, Makens, and Choy (Gee, Makens, James C., and Choy, Dexter J. L. 1997). Tourist industry business practices and strategies are drawn from The Travel Industry, Professional Travel Agency Management, and other professional publications (Gee et al. 1990). Selected government and private studies are referenced throughout the book. Research studies on Pacific islands completed by the author and other researchers provided insights on the pattern of tourism development for other tourist destinations within the Pacific region (D. J. Choy 1998; Center for Tourism Policy Studies 1990a; 1990b; D. J. L. Choy 1984).

Organization of Book

This book is organized into nine chapters. Following this introduction, Chapter 2 introduces tourism concepts and a review of world travel trends. Chapters 3-6 analyze the development of Hawaii's tourism within the framework of the product life cycle. Chapter 7 covers tourism planning and promotion in Hawaii. Chapter 8 analyzes lessons from past experience, current tourism issues, and Hawaii's tourism industry within the context of the Asia Pacific region. The book ends with recommendations for moving forward in the face of an uncertain future in Chapter 9.

Terminology

Terms are used in the text to refer to specific aspects of Hawaii and its tourism industry. The eight major islands of the Hawaiian Islands are Oahu, Maui, Kauai, island of Hawaii, Lanai, Molokai, Niihau, and Kahoolawe. The term *Neighbor Islands* typically refers to the seven major islands other than Oahu.

Figure 1.2: Hawaiian Islands
Source: Courtesy of FreeWorldMaps.net (https://www.freeworldmaps.net/united-states/hawaii/map.html)

In this book, *Neighbor Islands* is used to refer primarily to the three major islands other than Oahu i.e., Maui, Kauai and Hawaii island as shown in the map of the Hawaiian Islands. Kahoolawe is uninhabited. Niihau is privately owned, and no visitors are allowed except by permission of the owners. Lanai and Molokai account for only a small percentage of total visitors to Hawaii. Hawaii island also will be referred to as the *Big Island* to avoid confusion from referring to the State of Hawaii.

Within the context of Hawaii, the term *visitor* is used interchangeably with the term *tourist*. The data on visitors to Hawaii are for those who stay overnight or longer, and this is equivalent to the UNWTO definition of a tourist which is discussed in Chapter 2. The terms *U.S. mainland or mainland* are used to refer to the continental United States. Westbound travel to Hawaii is from origins east of Hawaii. Eastbound travel to Hawaii is from origins west of Hawaii and from Oceania traveling northeast to Hawaii. The term *Asia-Pacific region* refers to countries in Asia and Oceania.

Limitations of the Analysis

The analysis in this book focuses on key factors that affected Hawaii's tourism development as a whole and does not provide a detailed analysis of each island or every issue related to tourism. The intent is to create a historical discourse that emphasizes the major changes that influenced the different stages of Hawaii's tourism growth. It would be impossible to cover all issues which of themselves would deserve extended discussions and analysis. References are made throughout the book for readers to delve further into issues that are of interest to them. The events and data are presented in sequence to reveal underlying factors that brought about growth in Hawaii's tourism. Throughout the years, inquiries have been made to the School of TIM for a book on how tourism developed in Hawaii. Tourism professionals from other Asia-Pacific countries wanted to learn from Hawaii's experience to develop tourism in their respective countries. This book was written in response to those requests.

Limitations of an eBook

Most eBooks are done in a format that is reflowable where the contents of a page changes to automatically adjust to the screen size of the device that is being used to read the book. Limitations of the reflowable format are that text in multiple columns cannot be handled; tables may not display correctly; and footnotes are not widely supported. To overcome these limitations, figures, tables, and graphs are not used in this book. Instead, the analysis of relevant data is described in the narrative, focusing on key conclusions.

A printed second edition of the book will include figures, tables, and graphs for readers to visually follow the analysis. To avoid using footnotes, the Chicago Manual of Style 17th Edition, author-date system is used for citations. Detailed information on sources for the citations is available in the bibliography for interested readers. To facilitate the flow of the narrative, the citations are not linked to the bibliography.

Chapter 2
Tourism Concepts & World Travel Trends

Definition of Tourism

The terms *travel and tourism* often are used interchangeably. It, however, is important to distinguish the difference between travelers and tourists to understand the development of tourism and why people travel. Tourism and tourist are the more commonly used terms and usually refer to discretionary travel by people for leisure and recreational pursuits. Organizations at the world, country and state level have used different definitions of tourism. The internationally accepted definition of tourism and worldwide statistics on tourists encompass more than leisure and recreational pursuits. As defined by the UNWTO:

"Tourism is a social, cultural and economic phenomenon which entails the movement of people to countries or places outside their usual environment for personal or business/professional purposes. These people are called visitors (which may be either tourists or excursionists; residents or non-residents) and tourism has to do with their activities, some of which involve tourism expenditure" (UNWTO 2008, 1).

Non-resident travelers entering a country i.e., inbound travelers, are included in UNWTO statistics as traveling for a variety of reasons including business, leisure travel, visiting friends and relatives, education, health, religion, and shopping. Inbound travelers excluded from UNWTO statistics include border workers, seasonal workers, nomads, transit passengers, crews on public modes of transport, immigrants, diplomats, consular staff, and military. A complete listing is available in the UNWTO publication, *International Recommendations for Tourism Statistics 2008* (UNWTO 2010, 17).

Visiting friends and relatives (VFR) is a significant market segment for travel, but VFR usually is not considered when developing a tourist destination. The reason for this is that the destinations for VFR travelers are predetermined by the location of their friends and relatives. Tourists according to the UNWTO definition include visitors who stayed at least one night in the country entered. Same-day visitors who did not spend a night in the country are called excursionists (UNWTO 2010, 17). It should be noted that for the UNWTO definition of tourists, all the trip purposes listed for inbound travelers are included and not just leisure and recreational reasons.

In the United States, the term *travel* was preferred to *tourism* for developing government policies at the Federal government level. Most people in the United States associated tourism with primarily leisure and recreational travel. The term *travel* encompassed all forms of travel and was more inclusive than using the term *tourism* (Gee, Makens, James C., and Choy, Dexter J. L. 1997, p.11). The names of Federal government organizations such as the United States Travel and Tourism Administration (USTTA) and United States Travel Data Center (USTDC) reflected this preference. Although there was agreement that travel involved going outside a person's usual environment, the definition of non-local travel had to be made operational for measuring travel by Americans. The USTDC defined non-local travel as a trip extending one hundred miles or more from origin to destination (Gee, Makens, James C., and Choy, Dexter J. L. 1997, p.14). Daily routine trips such as commuting to and from work were excluded. Trip distances of fifty miles and twenty-five miles one-way have been used by other organizations to define non-local travel. The distance of one hundred miles for defining non-local travel is a realistic criterion for the United States, because fifty miles and twenty-five miles are short distances within a person's usual environment. For international travel, the parameter of trip distance is not part of the UNWTO definition. If a traveler crossed an international border for accepted trip purposes, he/she would be counted as a tourist.

In the early history of Hawaii, most of the travelers on sailing ships were in transit to destinations beyond Hawaii or immigrating to Hawaii. There were very few tourists to Hawaii until transportation to the islands improved and facilities to accommodate tourists were developed in the islands. As Hawaii gained popularity as a tourist destination, especially after World War II, most travelers were coming to visit the islands as tourists. Historical data on tourists to Hawaii included only visitors staying overnight or longer, which is consistent with the UNWTO definition of a tourist. The term *tourist* can have negative connotations, and Hawaii preferred to use the term *visitor* to refer to tourists visiting the islands. For example, the Hawaii Tourist Bureau (HTB) was formed in 1919 but was replaced by the Hawaii Visitors Bureau (HVB) in 1945 (Hawaii Visitors & Convention Bureau 2020, p.1).

Some confusion can arise from Hawaii's use of the term *visitor* to refer to tourists. According to the UNWTO definitions, visitors included both tourists and excursionists. Given the far distance from origin markets, border traffic by excursionists staying less than one day in Hawaii was never significant. Almost all visitors to Hawaii were tourists. Day tours became significant when cruises to and within the islands became popular. Data on cruise passengers are maintained separate from overnight or longer visitors. The analysis of Hawaii's tourism in this book includes only data on visitors by air and excludes cruise visitors, which comprise only a small portion of total visitors.

World Travel Trends

All of the data on international tourist arrivals, receipts and expenditures are from the UNWTO Tourism Data Dashboard (UNWTO 2018). UNWTO reports on international tourist arrivals measure the number of non-resident travelers visiting regions and countries throughout the world. Non-resident travelers are considered tourists because they have stayed overnight in the country that they visited. Since 1980, international tourist arrivals have increased five-fold from 276 million to 1.4 billion in 2018. Europe historically received the largest share of tourists due to border crossings between nearby countries. In 1980, Europe received over half, 61 percent, of all tourist arrivals, but its share of tourist arrivals declined to only half, 51 percent, in 2018.

The decline in Europe's dominance was due to the rapid growth of tourists to the Asia-Pacific region. Since 1980, tourist arrivals to the Asia-Pacific region increased fifteen-fold, from 23 million to 348 million in 2018. A significant reason for this rapid growth was the opening of China in 1978. By 2018, the Asia-Pacific region share of tourist arrivals almost doubled from 13 percent in 1980 to 25 percent in 2018. Similar to Europe, the Americas' share of tourist arrivals declined from 21 percent in 1980 to 15 percent in 2018. Africa and the Middle East combined receive less than 10 percent of international tourist arrivals world-wide.

UNWTO reports on international tourist receipts measure the amount of money that tourists spent in the countries that they visited. Europe's dominance in terms of international tourist receipts is much less than that for tourist arrivals. International tourist receipts for 2018 were equal to $1,462 billion. Although Europe received 51percent of tourist arrivals in 2018, it only received 39 percent of all tourist receipts. The Asia-Pacific region received 30 percent of all tourist receipts and the Americas received 23 percent of tourist receipts. The reason for Europe's decline in dominance in terms of tourist receipts is that Europe's receipts per arrival was only $800 compared to $1,570 for the Americas and $1,270 for the Asia-Pacific region. The lower receipts per arrival for Europe reflects the fact that approximately half of international travel to Europe is intra-regional travel between European countries. Whereas two-thirds of international travel to the Asia-Pacific region involves long-haul travel from Europe and the Americas; and three-fourths of the international travel to the Americas comes from far distance markets in Europe and the Asia-Pacific region (UNWTO 2018). People traveling long-haul to a destination tend to spend more at the destination than people traveling on short trips.

Regarding trip purpose, a little more than half – 56 percent of trips in 2018 – were for leisure, recreation, and sightseeing. One-fourth, 27 percent, of the trips were for VFR, health, religious, and other reasons; and one-tenth, 12 percent, were for business and professional reasons. The number of international business travelers tends to be underestimated. Business travelers typically will indicate that they are traveling for leisure purposes to avoid additional visa and customs requirements at international border crossings. If business travel is substantially more than estimated, trips made for leisure, recreation and sightseeing may be less than half of all trips. For developing tourist destinations, leisure travelers are usually thought of as the market segment that can be influenced by the attractiveness of an area because they have a choice in selecting the places to visit.

Major Destinations of the World

In 2018, the most popular destination in the world in terms of international tourist arrivals was France with almost ninety million tourists. Spain was the second most popular destination with 83 million tourists, followed by the United States with 80 million tourists, China with 63 million, and Italy with 62 million. These five destinations accounted for one-fourth, 27 percent, of all tourist arrivals in 2018. The next five most popular destinations were Turkey, Mexico, Germany, Thailand, and the United Kingdom, which together accounted for only one-seventh, 14 percent, of all arrivals. The UNWTO membership includes 158 countries and 6 territories. The degree of concentration in tourist arrivals can be seen in that the top ten destinations accounted for two out of every five or 41 percent of all tourist arrivals in 2018.

International tourist receipts measure the amount of money that a country receives from tourists visiting their respective countries. There also is a high degree of concentration when one considers international tourist receipts. The United States by far receives the most international tourist receipts compared to other countries. The United States' tourist receipts of $215 billion accounted for one-seventh, 15 percent, of total tourist receipts in 2018. Spain was the next country receiving the most tourist receipts with $74 billion, followed by France with $67 billion, Thailand with $63 billion and the United Kingdom with $52 billion. The top five countries accounted for one-third, 32 percent, of total tourist receipts and the top ten countries accounted for almost half, 47 percent, of all tourist receipts in 2018. Of the 164 countries and territories included in UNWTO data, only one sixteenth, 6 percent, received almost half of all tourist arrivals and receipts in 2018.

As opposed to the international tourist receipts that a country receives from tourists, international tourist expenditures measure the amount of money that residents of a country spend traveling abroad i.e., traveling outbound from their home country. International tourist expenditures for 2018 totaled $1,462 billion. Chinese tourists traveling abroad spent $277 billion on visits to other countries and were the top tourism spenders in 2018. Chinese tourists' expenditures on their visits to other countries was almost double the $144 billion spent by U.S. residents on international trips. Tourist expenditures by U.S. residents visiting other countries were ranked second to Chinese tourists' expenditures. German tourists were the third biggest spenders with $94 billion spent on international travel. These top three countries accounted for one-third, 35 percent, of total tourist expenditures for 2018.

The fourth biggest spenders were United Kingdom tourists with $76 billion spent on international travel, followed by French tourists spending $48 billion, Australian tourists spending $37 billion, Russian tourists $35 billion, Canadian tourists $33 billion, South Korean tourists $32 billion and Italian tourists $30 billion. Total expenditures for the top ten countries accounted for over half, 55 percent, of total tourist expenditures in 2018. From a world-wide perspective, these ten countries are key tourism markets in terms of expenditures of their residents traveling abroad. Other factors, however, such as distance to a destination, travel time, personal preferences and the reason for traveling can have an equal or larger influence on a person's choice of a destination than monetary considerations.

Asia-Pacific Travel Trends

As stated previously in Chapter 1, the term *Asia-Pacific region* is used in this book to refer to countries in Asia and Oceania. Many maps of the world are centered on the Atlantic Ocean due to the historic focus on travel between Europe and the Americas, and the use of the Mercator projection for maps. The map of the world showing the Pacific Ocean in the center provides a different perspective of the world with Asian countries across the vast Pacific Ocean from the Americas and only the Atlantic coastlines of a few European countries being visible.

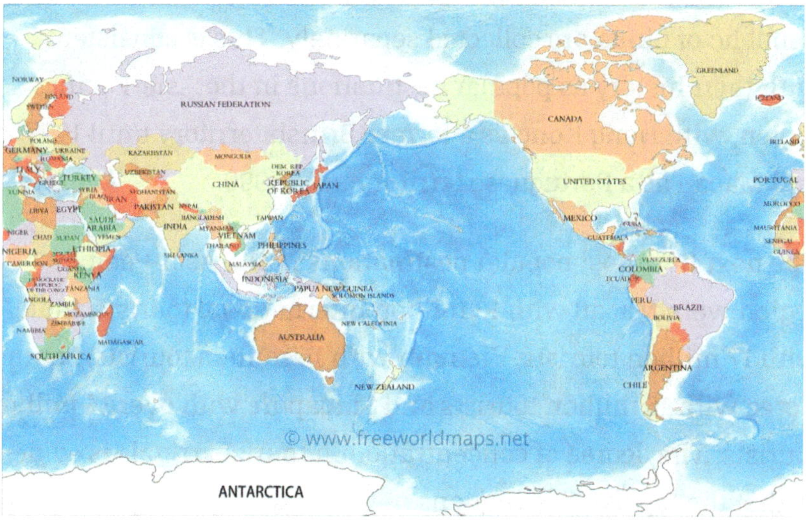

Figure 2.1: Pacific-Centered World Map
Source: Courtesy of FreeWorldMaps.net (https://www.freeworldmaps.net/world/pacific-centered/pacific-centered-countries-worldmap.jpg)

The Pacific–centered map is more relevant than an Atlantic–centered map to the analysis of the development of tourism in Hawaii. Early visitors used Hawaii as a stopover point on their voyages across the Pacific. Major tourist markets to Hawaii originate primarily from North America and Asia.

In 2018, international tourist arrivals to the Asia-Pacific region totaled 348 million. The most popular destination in the Asia-Pacific region was China with 63 million international tourists in 2018. China's dominance in the Asia-Pacific region would be expected given its world ranking as the fourth most popular destination. The number of tourists to China was almost double that of any other destination in the region. The second most popular destination was Thailand with 38 million tourists, followed by Japan with 31 million tourists, Hong Kong with 29 million, and Malaysia with 26 million. Data on Hong Kong and Macau as Special Administrative Regions of the People's Republic of China are collected separately. This is consistent with their history as popular destinations in the Asia-Pacific region, with Hong Kong as a former British territory until 1997 and Macau as a Portuguese territory until 1999.

The next five most popular destinations in the Asia-Pacific region were Macau with 18 million international tourists, India with 17 million tourists, Vietnam with 16 million tourists, South Korea with 15 million tourists and Singapore with over 14 million tourists. The degree of concentration in tourist arrivals is evident in that the top five destinations in the Asia-Pacific region account for over half, 54 percent, of total international tourist arrivals in the region, and the top ten destinations account for over three-fourths, 77 percent, of total international tourist arrivals for the region.

Total international tourist receipts for the Asia-Pacific region were equal to $442 billion in 2018. Although China was the most popular destination in terms of tourist arrivals, it only ranked fourth in terms of international tourist receipts for the region. Thailand received the most international tourist receipts with $63 billion, followed by Australia with $45 billion and Japan with $41 billion. Macau's tourist receipts ranked fifth and were almost equal to China's tourist receipts of $40 billion. The next five countries receiving the most international tourist receipts were Hong Kong with $38 billion, India with $29 billion, Singapore with $21 billion, Malaysia $19 billion and South Korea $15 billion. The top five destinations accounted for half, 52 percent, of total international tourist receipts in the Asia-Pacific region and tourist receipts for the top ten destinations accounted for almost four-fifths, 79 percent, of total international tourist receipts for the region.

In terms of international tourist expenditures, Chinese tourists dominate the Asia-Pacific region as the top spender with $277 million spent on international travel in 2018. This amount was more than the combined total for the remaining nine countries as the top spenders in the Asia-Pacific region. Australian tourists were the second biggest spenders with $37 billion spent on international travel; followed by South Korean tourists spending $32 billion, Japanese tourists spending $28 billion, and Hong Kong tourists spending $27 billion. The remaining five of the top ten spenders in the Asia-Pacific region were Indian tourists spending $26 billion, Singaporean tourists spending $23 billion, Thai tourists $15 billion, Malaysian tourists $13 billion and Filipino tourists $12 billion.

Not all the spending by Chinese tourists was on visits to Asia-Pacific destinations. Nevertheless, the top destinations of Chinese tourists for 2018 were in the Asia-Pacific region, including Thailand, Japan, Vietnam, Singapore, Indonesia, Malaysia, Cambodia, and the Philippines. Hong Kong and Macau also were among the most visited destinations by Chinese tourists.

Oceania Travel Trends

As shown in the map of Oceania, the area includes fourteen countries: Australia, Micronesia, Fiji, Kiribati, Marshall Islands, Nauru, New Zealand, Palau, Papua New Guinea, Samoa, Solomon Islands, Tonga, Tuvalu, and Vanuatu. Oceania also includes islands which are states, territories, or islands with political links to major countries. Hawaii, American Samoa, Guam, and the Northern Mariana Islands are part of the United States. French Polynesia and New Caledonia are French overseas territories. The Cook Islands has political links with New Zealand, and Pitcairn Islands is a British overseas territory. Oceania encompasses Australasia, Melanesia, Micronesia, and Polynesia, and covers an area of 3.3 million square miles.

UNWTO data on tourist arrivals and receipts in Oceania include territories such as Guam and French Polynesia. However, international tourists to Hawaii are not counted separately from data on the United States. In 2018, international tourist arrivals to Oceania totaled 17 million, which accounted for only one percent of international tourist arrivals worldwide and only five percent of international tourist arrivals to the Asia-Pacific region.

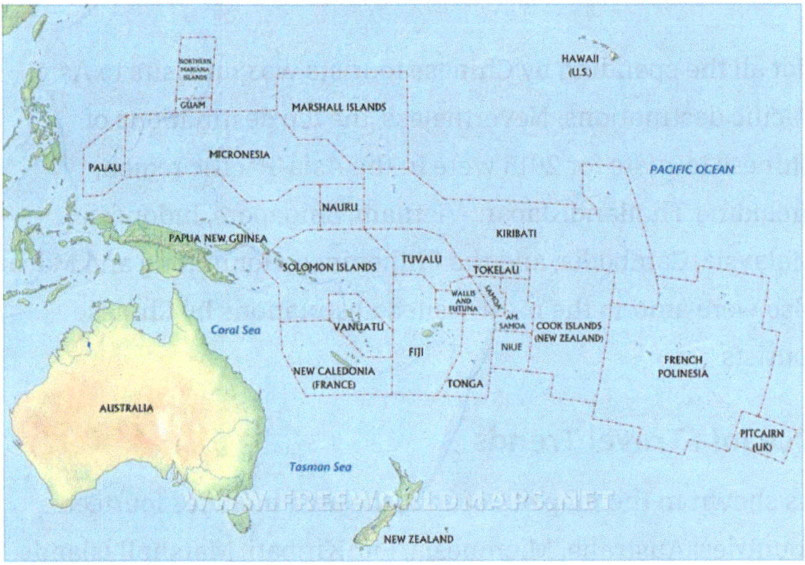

Figure 2.2: Oceania
Source: Courtesy of Freeworldmaps.net (https://www.freeworldmaps.net/oceania/)

Australia and New Zealand accounted for three-fourths, 76 percent, of international tourist arrivals to Oceania. Excluding New Zealand, the eighteen Pacific islands included in UNWTO data accounted for only four million international tourist arrivals in 2018. The combined international tourist arrivals of the other eighteen islands included in UNWTO data comprised a marginal share, 1 percent, of international tourist arrivals to the Asia-Pacific region, which in turn would be negligible relative to international tourist arrivals worldwide.

The rapid growth in international tourist arrivals to the Asia-Pacific region, thus, reflects the increase in tourists to Asian destinations more so than Pacific Island destinations. The main exception to this would be the growth of tourists to Hawaii, which is not reported in UNWTO data. Hawaii's tourism industry within the context of the Asia-Pacific region is analyzed in Chapter 8.

Models of Destination Development

The previous discussion of world travel trends was primarily at the macro and regional levels. Models of a destination's development have been researched at the regional level in regard to specific areas such as Europe, individual countries, and states, and at the micro level on individual resorts. The concept of a resort or destination life cycle was recognized over thirty years ago. In one of the first books on modern tourism, Likorish and Kershaw described how the seaside resorts in Britain first were discovered by wealthy tourists; grew in popularity with the advent of middle-income tourists; and then declined as lower income tourists replaced middle-income tourists (Lickorish 1958, 24–26). Christaller proposed a development cycle for destinations in Europe in which a destination is initially discovered by painters and artists; becomes fashionable; and eventually is visited by only tourists on package tours (Christaller 1964, 103). Plog's theory on the rise and fall of destinations related the popularity of tourist destinations to the personality types of travelers (Plog 1974).

Butler was the first to suggest a specific pattern of development for a destination. Butler proposed that the growth in arrivals to a tourist destination followed the S-shaped curve of the product life cycle (Butler 1980, 6–10). The conventional stages of the product life cycle are introduction, growth, maturity, and decline. Butler described six stages through which a destination evolves: exploration, involvement, development, consolidation, stagnation, and decline/rejuvenation. Butler's characterization of the stages, however, appears to be more hypothetical than empirically based. Empirical studies reveal a variety of product life cycle shapes.

A study on Pacific Island destinations showed that the S-shaped curve of the product life cycle model did not apply to most Pacific Island destinations (Choy 1992, 29–31). For Hawaii, the S-shaped curve was generally representative of the growth in visitors to Hawaii up until the 1990s, when stagnation in visitor arrivals occurred.

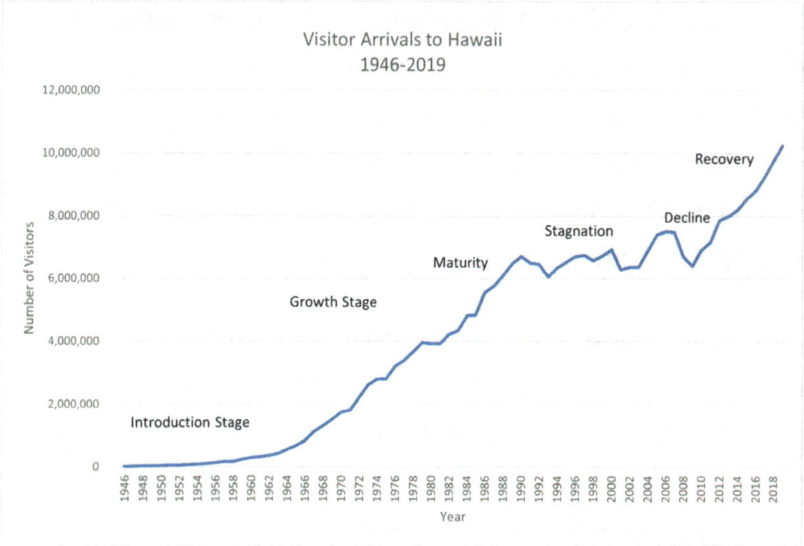

Figure 2.3: Hawaii's Tourism Life Cycle
Source: Data from the State of Hawaii, Dept. of Business, Economic Development & Tourism

As shown in Figure 2.3, the pattern of visitor arrivals to Hawaii from 1946-2019 went through six stages: introduction, growth, maturity, stagnation, decline and recovery. Although not shown in the graph, the analysis of the introduction stage in Chapter 3 goes further back in history to 1785. The criterion for delineating the stages for Hawaii's tourism life cycle also is discussed in Chapter 3.

Summary

World-wide tourism trends reveal a high degree of concentration in international tourist arrivals and tourist receipts. Regarding destinations, ten countries accounted for almost half of tourist arrivals and receipts. In terms of international tourist expenditures, the residents from ten countries accounted for half of total tourist expenditures on travel abroad. The degree of concentration was even higher for the Asia-Pacific region with China being a major destination as well as the top spender on international travel. On a world-wide and regional basis, the Pacific islands account for only a marginal amount of tourist arrivals except for Hawaii. A void in the rankings of top destinations in the world is the absence of any Pacific Island. Australia was the only country in Oceania ranking among the top world destinations in terms of receipts.

In analyzing Hawaii's development and growth, the UNWTO definitions of international tourists and USTDC. definition of a trip will be used to define tourists to Hawaii. The product life cycle model will be used as a framework for analyzing the life cycle stages of Hawaii's tourism. Patterns of growth and strategies, both successful and unsuccessful, will be identified within the context of Hawaii as well as the experience of other destinations in the Asia-Pacific region. The focus will be on factors that contributed to the growth of Hawaii's tourism. A discussion on the social, cultural, and environmental impacts of tourism will be offered in the context of destination management in Chapter 9.

Chapter 3

Introduction & Early Growth Stages: Tourism Before Statehood

Stages of Hawaii's Early Development

The history of Hawaii before statehood can be divided into different time periods. Kuykendall identifies six time periods: 1) Ancient Hawaii to 1779; 2) Evolution of a Constitutional Kingdom 1778-1854; 3) The Middle Period of Change 1854-1874; 4) Later Years of the Kingdom 1874-1893; 5) Hawaii in Transition 1894-1900; and 6) Hawaii from Territory to Statehood 1900-1959 (Kuykendall 1961, vii–viii). Kuykendall portrays how Hawaii was transformed into a modern economy and society within a relatively short time. During the later time periods, Hawaii's prosperity was primarily from trade, industry, and agriculture. Kuykendall's analysis coincides with the early stages of economic growth characterized by W. M. Rostow.

In his theory of economic growth, Rostow encompasses the social and political changes that are necessary to achieve economic growth. Based upon the experience of industrialized countries, Rostow delineates five stages of growth: 1) Traditional Society; 2) Pre-Conditions for Take-Off; 3) Take-Off; 4) Drive to Maturity and 5) Age of High Mass Consumption (Rostow 1960). The first stage, Traditional Society, corresponds to Kuykendall's Ancient Hawaii. The second stage, Preconditions to Growth, encompasses the social and political changes that must occur for economic growth to be attained and corresponds to Kuykendall's second, third and fourth periods in Hawaii's history. Once Hawaii became part of the United States, the resources necessary for Hawaii's economy to take off were readily available from the United States. With annexation in 1898 and territorial status in 1900, Hawaii's development was linked to that of the United States as described in Kuykendall's last two time periods.

Chong identifies three stages of tourist related activities prior to 1945. The first stage was marked by the construction of the Hawaiian Hotel in 1872. The second stage was a period of expansion in tourist plant capacity from 1898-1903; and the third stage was the 1920s (Chong 1963, chap. V–VII). Crampon provides an intricate account of early travel to Hawaii and tourist related activity but did not complete his analysis beyond the 1920s (Crampon 1973). Although information from previous studies is integrated into the analysis, this book adopts a different perspective.

The time periods used in this chapter are based upon the changes in transportation modes to Hawaii as demarcation points for analyzing the early development of Hawaii's tourism. Efficient transportation is critical for the success of a destination. Transportation companies historically have developed lodging facilities along their routes to accommodate passengers and resorts at scenic sites to attract passengers. Development of facilities at destinations have been done in response to the potential impact of new transportation services. In addition, the characteristics of the mode of transportation such as comfort, speed, convenience, and cost are barriers to travel and significantly influence travel patterns. The changes in transportation modes to Hawaii during the years covered in this chapter were sailing ships, steamship transportation and early air travel with propeller planes up to the introduction of jet aircraft.

Hawaii as a Port of Call: Sailing Ships 1785–1866

During the 1700s, the average speed of sailing ships was four to six knots per hour. A sailing ship could travel about 100–140 miles per day (Caird Library 2012). Based on this speed, it would have taken three weeks or more to travel from San Francisco to Honolulu. A two-week vacation in the islands would require eight or more weeks, including the roundtrip. It was unlikely for someone to spend less time in the islands than it took to travel roundtrip from San Francisco. One would surmise that travelers to Hawaii would stay in the islands about a month or more.

Sailing ships were primarily designed to carry crew and cargo. Tourism during this time was typically an outcome of commercial activities using the islands as a transit point. Commercial activities affecting the Hawaiian economy changed throughout the years. From 1785–1810, fur traders crossing the Pacific to Canton used Hawaii as a port to replenish supplies. At about the same time, sandalwood was being harvested in Hawaii and shipped to China from 1791 until 1830, when the sandalwood was depleted (Kuykendall 1961, 30–32, 42–43).

The first whaling ships stopped to replenish supplies in 1819. Whaling peaked in 1846 and ceased to be of any importance by 1876 (Kuykendall 1961, 117–18). It was during the height of the whaling industry in the Pacific that the number of merchant and whaling ships calling at Hawaii reached 706 ships in 1850 (Crampon 1973, 101,104A). Very few, if any, passengers were carried on the whaling ships since their primary objective was to go beyond Hawaii to hunt for whales. Boarding houses and crude hotels were built in downtown Honolulu to accommodate the crews of the ships. The traders and whaling crews would be considered tourists according to UNWTO definitions. Traders and whaling crews as part of business travel often precede the advent of leisure travelers to new, unknown destinations when they hear about faraway exotic places from business travelers returning home. Business travelers also often form the basis upon which transportation companies can open new routes.

As interest in visiting the islands increased through commerce and communications, facilities for passengers were added to merchant ships. Passengers on the ships were accommodated as by-products of the cargo being shipped. Travel by sailing ship was unreliable due to delays caused by weather and equipment failures. The trip was uncomfortable and having to travel three weeks or more to reach Honolulu limited the appeal of visiting the islands. Whaling declined through the 1860s, resulting in a substantial decline in ships visiting Hawaiian ports. Crampon estimated that the number of visitors declined from a peak of 14,100 in 1859 to a low of 2,100 in 1862 (Crampon 1973, 128). From this decline, it is evident that most of the visitors during this period were the crews of the whaling ships.

Steamship Service 1867–1934

Regular steamship service between San Francisco and Hawaii was introduced by the Pacific Mail Steamship Company in 1867 with a mail subsidy from the U.S. government (Chong 1963, 58–

59). Travel by steamship from San Francisco to Honolulu could be done in eight to ten days (The Maritime Heritage Project 2020). Steamships were more reliable than sailing ships and the trip was more comfortable. The substantial reduction in travel time made it less taxing to visit the islands. A tourist could travel to Hawaii and stay for two weeks with the total trip taking a little more than a month compared to traveling by sailing ship, which required two months or more for a two–week visit in Hawaii.

Earlier articles by Mark Twain writing for a California newspaper were widely read and began to generate public interest in visiting the islands. From the low of 2,100 visitors in 1862, the number of visitors tripled to 6,200 in 1866 (Crampon 1973, 128). A significant proportion of these visitors were thought to be tourists traveling for pleasure. Whether in transit to destinations beyond Hawaii or to Hawaii as the final destination, passengers on the steamships were tourists requiring better facilities than the boarding houses and crude hotels built for traders and crews of the whaling ships as exemplified in the picture of the Globe Hotel. The Globe Hotel was formerly the home of Hannah Holmes, daughter of Oliver Holmes. The hotel was built mostly of coral stone, it was located on King and Fort Streets.

Figure 3.1: Globe Hotel 1850
Source: Hawaii State Archives, Date: Ca 1850; Photographer: R.J. Baker

Recognizing the potential need for better tourist accommodations, the Hawaiian government built the Hawaiian Hotel in 1872. The construction was primarily financed by bonds issued by the Hawaiian government, which at the time was a constitutional monarchy. The hotel was located at the corner of Richards and Hotel Street where the Hawaii State Art Museum currently is located. The hotel had forty-two rooms and could accommodate sixty to ninety guests. It had a cottage at Waikiki Beach for guests to enjoy spending a day at the beach. As concluded by Chong, "*the Hawaiian Hotel was the first effort to establish first-class facilities in Hawaii, the first instance of government participation in stimulating tourism to Hawaii, and the first large- scale example of a tourist-oriented establishment providing substantial employment to a rising domestic population*" (Chong 1963, Chap. V).

The picture of the Hawaiian Hotel shows the elegance of the hotel compared to the boarding houses and crude hotels built for traders and crews. With its location right across Iolani Barracks and later Iolani Palace built in 1882, the Hawaiian Hotel was convenient for foreign dignitaries and business travelers. Downtown Honolulu with Honolulu Harbor nearby was the center of commercial activity. Waikiki was an auxiliary site for guests to only enjoy the beach because the surrounding area was not developed as it is today. It would not be until the 1920s that the land area now referred to as Waikiki was reclaimed for development. Despite an upward trend in arrivals, the early years of the Hawaiian Hotel's operations were unprofitable, and after ten years, the government awarded the lease to another person to manage the hotel (Crampon 1973, 180–83).

Figure 3.2: Hawaiian Hotel
Source: Hawaii State Archives, Date: ca. 1890

In 1875, the Pacific Mail Steamship Company extended it services from San Francisco to Australia and New Zealand via Honolulu (Chong 1963, 59). Recognizing the growth in tourist traffic, the company built new ships that had sleeping cabins for first-class passengers. Lesser accommodations were available for second-class and third-class passengers. The cabins for first- class passengers were well appointed and were located near a spacious dining room. The construction of elaborate facilities for passengers reflected the higher class of tourists that were traveling on the long route.

The Treaty of Reciprocity in 1876 between Hawaii and the U.S. government increased the ties between Hawaii's sugar industry and the mainland United States (Kuykendall 1961, 152). The treaty in 1887 to use Pearl Harbor extended the ties to the U.S. military (Kuykendall 1961, 160). In 1888, King Kalakaua granted a royal charter to publish *Paradise of the Pacific* magazine to promote Hawaii to the world (Honolulu Magazine 2020, 1). Hawaii also was being promoted as a health resort with the clean air and restful atmosphere of the islands. Trans-Pacific travel to Hawaii was increasing due to increased commercial activity and the growth of tourist markets on the West Coast of the U.S. mainland. The Spanish American War, which began in April 1898, brought thousands of American soldiers transiting Hawaii to the Philippines (Chong 1963, 115–16). A few months after the war began, the United States annexed Hawaii, which was the first step in the process for Hawaii to become a permanent part of the United States (Kuykendall 1961, 189).

The Oahu Rail & Land Company (OR&L) built the Haleiwa Hotel in 1899 at the end of the railroad line in Haleiwa, Oahu. The hotel was built to attract visitors and Honolulu residents to travel by train to Haleiwa and stay at the hotel to enjoy the beach and surrounding natural beauty (Chong 1963, 117–18). The picture of the Haleiwa Hotel shows that the owners designed the hotel at a similar level of luxury as the Hawaiian Hotel.

Figure 3.3: Haleiwa Hotel, Haleiwa, Oahu
Source: Hawaii State Archives

OR&L building the hotel at the end of their rail line followed the strategy of railroad companies in other parts of the world that built hotels and resorts along their routes to attract passengers to ride their trains. The Haleiwa Hotel was part of OR&L's plan to diversify the operations of the railroad. As automobiles became prevalent in the 1920s as the primary means of traveling around the island, travel by train declined and the Haleiwa Hotel eventually closed.

On the San Francisco to Honolulu route, Oceanic Steamship Company launched three steamships from 1900–1901 with increased passenger capacity (Chong 1963, chap. III). The ships still were primarily for cargo but included several hundred first-class cabins as well as facilities for second-class and third-class passengers. In anticipation of increases in the number of tourists, two first-class hotels were built: the Moana Hotel in 1901 and the Alexander Young Hotel in 1903 (Chong 1963, chap. VII).

The Moana Hotel was the first luxury hotel built in Waikiki with seventy-five rooms. The picture of the Moana Hotel shows how elegant it was, towering five stories above the main street running through Waikiki. The Alexander Young Hotel was the largest hotel in Hawaii with accommodations for three hundred guests. The Alexander Young Hotel was in downtown Honolulu, which was still the main area for tourist activity.

Figure 3.4: Moana Hotel, Waikiki
Source: Hawaii State Archives, Date: ca. 1908

The large increase in the number of hotel rooms coincided with the establishment of the Hawaii Promotion Committee in 1903 to advertise Hawaii to the U.S. mainland. The Committee received a $15,000 appropriation, which was matched by private sources of funding (Hawaii Visitors & Convention Bureau 2020). Matson Navigation Company, founded in 1901, launched its first steamship on the San Francisco to Hawaii route in 1902. Showing interest in competing for tourist traffic, Matson launched the *Lurline II* in 1908 with capacity for 50 passengers (Chong 1963, chap. III). Even with organized promotion and increased passenger capacity by Oceanic and Matson, the hotel construction boom resulted in over capacity and operating losses. Consolidation in the hotel industry occurred when the

Moana Hotel and Hawaiian Hotel were sold to Alexander Young's Territorial Hotel Company (Chong 1963, 121, 127).

Tourist facilities also were being built on the neighbor islands. The beginnings of a Volcano House date back to 1844 when Benjamin Pittman built a grass hut on the slopes of Mauna Kea (Crampon 1973, chap. VI). The picture of the Volcano House in 1861 shows a larger grass covered structure that replaced the original grass hut. The volcano on the island of Hawaii was a major attraction of Hawaii. Upgraded facilities were built during the mid-1860s and advertised as the Volcano House.

Figure 3.5: Volcano House, Hawaii Island
Source: Hawaii State Archives, Date: 1861

Inter-island transportation improved with the establishment of the Hawaiian Steam Navigation Company in 1859, followed by Wilder Steamship Company in 1877 and Inter-Island Steam

Navigation Company in 1882 (Chong 1963, chap. III). With the expansion of inter-island steamship service and introduction of passenger capacity on the ships, hotels were built on Kauai, Maui, and the island of Hawaii to accommodate tourists, but Honolulu was still the major tourist destination (Hawaii Hotel Association 1990).

During the early 1900s, Matson Navigation Company continued to increase passenger capacity on the San Francisco to Honolulu route by launching four passenger-freight combination ships. The *Wilhelmina*, with capacity for 146 passengers, was launched in 1910; the *Manoa*, with capacity for 90 passengers, in 1914; the *Matsonia* in 1914 and Maui in 1917, each with capacity for 252 passengers (Chong 1963, chap. III). Matson recognized the potential of increased passenger revenues, and the last two ships had more than double the passenger capacity of the *Manoa*. During the First World War (WWI), Hawaii was promoted as a safe destination since the war was being fought in Europe. The flow of traffic to Hawaii was disrupted when the Matson fleet was diverted to the Atlantic to support the war effort in Europe (Matson 2020, 3). Annual passenger traffic to Hawaii during WWI hovered around 30,000 but the majority, as much as 80%, were just passing through Hawaii (Chong 1963, 130). After the war ended, passengers visiting Hawaii staying at least one night began to increase and reached pre-war levels within a few years.

Although not part of tourist related activity, it is important to consider the impact of immigration resulting from the growth of the sugar industry. The first successful sugar plantation began on Kauai in 1835 (Kuykendall 1961, 92–93). More plantations were established following the Great Mahele in 1846 as foreigners were able to purchase land (Kuykendall 1961, 70–71). The Treaty of Reciprocity produced a boom in the sugar industry. The two largest sources of immigrant labor for the sugar plantations were from China and Japan, followed by immigrants from the Philippines in later years.

Available data on immigration show that immigrants from China increased from 364 in 1853 to a peak of 21,741 in 1900 and declined to 11,164 in 1920. The total number of immigrants from China during the years covered was over 100,000. Immigrants from Japan increased from 116 in 1884 to a peak of 60,690 in 1920. The total number of immigrants from Japan during the years covered was over 210,000. Available data on immigrants from the Philippines for 1910 and 1920 suggest that over 7,000 immigrants came from the Philippines (Schmitt 1977, 90). Not all immigrants were laborers, but the flow of large numbers of immigrants began with the sugar planters importing labor to work on their plantations and then followed by the pineapple industry importing labor to work on the pineapple fields.

Immigrants are excluded from data on tourists; however, immigration influences the pattern and growth of future travel by increasing the connections between countries. Commercial travel usually increases as business activity between countries increase. VFR travel increases as family and friends visit the countries where their relatives have immigrated. Subsequent generations not only continue visiting friends and relatives, but also are interested in sightseeing throughout the country to which their ancestors immigrated. Immigration thus provides the basis for a significant amount of travel between countries, or in this case, travel between Hawaii and Asia. The business, VFR and leisure travelers stemming from immigration would be considered tourists and become important sources of tourism over the years.

The transpacific routes between Hawaii and the U.S. mainland were the main sources of tourists during the 1920s. The event that changed the landscape forever was the building of the Reclamation Canal, now known as the Ala Wai Canal, in 1922 (Chong 1963, 132). The canal was built to drain the area which we now know as Waikiki and led to the further development of Waikiki as the major tourist center. With increased tourist traffic on its ships, Matson Navigation Company built the Royal Hawaiian Hotel in 1927 (Chong 1963, 136–37). The picture of the hotel shows that it was a six-story structure with 400 rooms providing luxurious accommodations for Matson passengers on the beach of Waikiki.

Figure 3.6: Royal Hawaiian Hotel 1927
Source: Hawaii State Archives

In the same year that the Royal Hawaiian Hotel opened, Matson launched the *Malolo*, which was the most technologically advanced and luxurious passenger ship at the time (Matson 2020, 3). It was the first pure passenger ship on the Hawaii to the U.S. mainland routes. Cruising at twenty-two knots, the *Malolo* could travel from San Francisco to Honolulu in about five days. A two-week vacation would take only about three weeks, including the roundtrip to Hawaii. The reduction in travel time and the luxurious on-board accommodations and services made a vacation to Hawaii convenient and comfortable for tourists from the West Coast of the United States. With the success of the *Malolo*, Matson built three additional luxury liners– the *Mariposa*, *Monterey* and *Lurline*. Matson painted all of the ships white as part of the romantic image created in traveling to Hawaii and the South Pacific (Matson 2020, 3–4).

Matson Navigation Company played a significant role in fostering the tourism industry during the 1900s. By the time that the *Malolo* was launched, Matson had acquired an interest in the Inter-Island Steam Navigation Company, which owned the Volcano House, and later the Kona Inn (Chong 1963, 138–40). These hotels were the only first-class hotels located on the Neighbor Islands. Matson also had acquired a controlling interest in the Territorial Hotel Company, which owned the Alexander Young Hotel, Moana Hotel, and the Seaside Cottages & Hotel. In addition, Matson operated a sightseeing company called the Royal Hawaiian Transport Company and owned the Waialae Golf Course. Through these acquisitions, Matson could offer an inclusive tour of the islands covering all major attractions. To promote travel to the islands, Matson undertook an advertising campaign using famous photographers and commissioned artists to design keepsake menus for the ships and the Royal Hawaiian Hotel, which are valued till today (Matson 2020, 4).

Figure 3.7: Matson's Aloha menu cover with an ukulele surrounded by a lei and native Hawaiian flowers in the background.
Source: Courtesy of Lorrin King

During the later years of the 1920s, visitors to Hawaii increased from 17,500 in 1927 to 22,200 in 1929. The stock market crash in October 1929 followed by the Great Depression of the 1930s resulted in four consecutive years of decline in visitors. It was not until 1934 that the number of visitors began to increase and showed signs of recovery (Schmitt 1977, 273). The pre-depression peak would not be reached until the next stage of transportation development across the Pacific.

Transpacific Air Travel–Propeller Aircraft 1935–1958

The first transpacific flight occurred in 1925 when a naval officer crossed the Pacific in a seaplane to Hawaii. Commercial flights between the Hawaiian Islands began in 1929 with the formation of Inter-Island Airways by Inter-Island Steamship Company (Hawaii Aviation 2015). Commercial transpacific flights began later in 1935 when Pan Am inaugurated the first airmail flight across the Pacific with a Martin M-130, later to be known as the China Clipper.

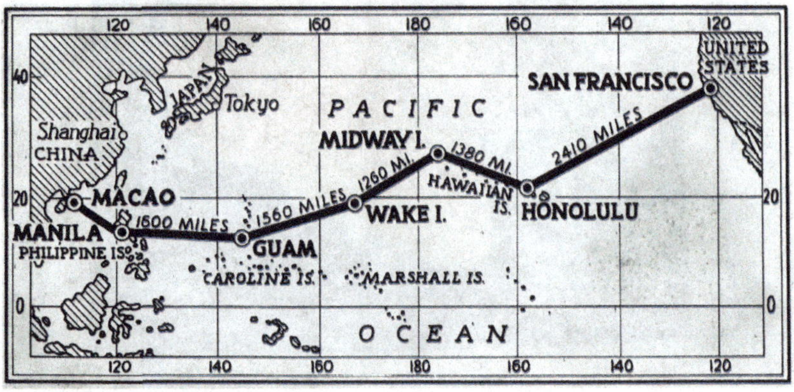

Figure 3.8: Pan American route from San Francisco to China.
Source: Smithsonian National Air and Space Museum (NASM 9A10460-020-X)

The flight from San Francisco to Honolulu took 21 hours and 20 minutes. The flight was only the first leg in Pan American's plans to cross the Pacific, with stopovers in Midway Island, Wake Island and Guam on its way to Manila as shown in the historic map above. The flight was later extended to Macau and Hong Kong (Pan Am Clipper Flying Boats 2020, 4).

As Pan American flew mail and freight across the Pacific, it also built hotels and passenger facilities on Midway and Wake Island. Passenger flights were inaugurated in 1936, with weekly passenger flights from San Francisco to Manila via Honolulu. The China Clippers were flying airboats that did not need an airstrip to land because they could land on water. Landing on water made it safer for crossing the Pacific, which had some of the longest air routes without any intermediate stops.

The China Clippers were amazingly comfortable with a lounge, dining room, and sleeping berths. A picture of a Pan American Clipper flying over Waikiki with Diamond Head in the background is given below. Only eight to ten passengers typically could be carried on a flight, because cargo and air mail were the priority (Aviation History Online Museum 2020, 2). Pan American received a government subsidy to transport mail across the Pacific like the mail subsidy received by the Pacific Mail Steamship Company.

Figure 3.9: Pan American Clipper flying over Waikiki with Diamond Head in the background
Source: Hawaii State Archives, Date: ca. 1935, Photographer: Pan-Pacific Press Bureau

Government subsidies to support the development of an industry are common in the United States as well as other countries. In addition to subsidies, government regulation often is used to foster an orderly growth of an industry. In the case of the U.S. airline industry, Congress passed the Civil Aviation Act of 1938, establishing the Civil Aeronautics Authority, which was known as the Civil Aeronautics Board (CAB) (Mola 2020). The functions of the CAB were to promote and regulate the U.S. airline industry. The CAB promoted the airline industry directly through subsidies and indirectly through its policies to encourage development of an adequate air transportation system. Through its certification powers, the CAB controlled entry into the U.S. airline industry as well as into specific origin-destination airline routes (Douglas 1974, 150–69, 197–205). Its control over air routes to Hawaii had major impacts upon travel to Hawaii. The CAB regulation of the

U.S. airline industry lasted two decades past statehood as will be discussed in the next chapter.

Pan American in 1939 introduced a new seaplane, the Boeing 314, which was much larger and more luxurious than the Martin M-130 (Boeing 2021). It was described as a flying hotel. The only class available was first class. Due to the priority given to mail and freight, only twenty-five passengers could be accommodated on a flight. The Boeing 314 had a longer range of 5,200 miles compared to the 3,200 miles range of the Martin M-130. With the Boeing 314, Pan American was able to develop a route to New Zealand via Hawaii and Canton Island. By 1941, the flying time between the West Coast and Hawaii was 16–18 hours. Although travel time by plane was less than a day compared to ship travel, the limited passenger capacity on the seaplanes meant that ship travel would remain the major means of travel from the West Coast to Hawaii up to World War II.

With the bombing of Pearl Harbor and America entering the war, tourist travel to the islands was curtailed. Matson's fleet of ships was commandeered for the war effort, and the Royal Hawaiian Hotel was used by the military (Matson 2020, 5). Matson had financial interests in the airline industry through Inter-Island Airways and in Pan American up to 1941. Matson had plans to enter the airline industry directly but was interrupted by the war. In 1943, Matson formed an Air Transport Division which provided maintenance and overhaul for naval aircraft. The Division had large operations in California (Dean 2015, 134–35). When the war ended, the Air Transport Division began to convert military aircraft for civilian use by Northwest Airlines and many other airlines.

Matson Airlines was formed in 1946 to provide nonscheduled service between the U.S. mainland and Hawaii using the type of aircraft that its Air Transport Division had converted to civilian use (Edwards 1994, 17–18). From the success of Inter-Island Airways, Matson recognized that travel across the Pacific eventually would be dominated by air travel. Matson applied for certification from the Civil Aeronautics Board to provide regular airline services from the U.S. mainland to Hawaii but was denied by the CAB. Matson Airlines continued flying between the U.S. mainland and Hawaii until the CAB granted route authority to United Airlines to fly from San Francisco to Honolulu, and Northwest Airlines to fly from Seattle and Portland to Honolulu (Melendy 2003, 203–6).

WWII brought changes that would affect Hawaii's tourism for many years to come. Like the Spanish American War, WWII brought thousands of military personnel from all branches to Hawaii, either to travel further to fight the war in the Pacific or to be stationed in Hawaii. In addition, civilian personnel supporting the war effort came to the islands. Soon after the end of WWII, the Korean War from June 1950 to July 1953 brought troops and civilian personnel to Hawaii. Wars fought in the Asia-Pacific region have had a significant impact on travel to the islands. Till this day, the bombing of Pearl Harbor is commemorated each year in Hawaii with veterans and their families traveling to attend the ceremony.

A major change in air transportation brought about by WWII was the use of larger aircraft to transport troops across the Atlantic Ocean. The C-54 Skymaster Transport was the military version of the DC-4 commercial passenger airplane. Thousands of troops and other personnel became familiar with flying. The ending of WWII resulted in a surplus of airplanes and flight crews that provided a foundation for expanding the airline industry to meet the increased demand for air travel after the war.

Pan American replaced the China Clippers with the DC-4 airplane and in 1946 was offering daily flights between the West Coast to Hawaii. The flight took about 12 1/2 hours (National Air & Space Museum 2020). With a standard seating of forty-four passengers, fares were lower than that of the China Clippers. By 1947, three-fourths of transpacific travel to Hawaii was by air. Continued improvements in aircraft speed and passenger capacity resulted in decreases in flying time to only eight hours from the West Coast. Tourists to Hawaii could celebrate Aloha Week and follow the visitor guides printed by the HVB to scenic sites around the islands marked by HVB "warrior markers". The first Aloha Week Court in 1947 is shown in the picture with the Aloha Week king and queen in native clothes and headdress.

Figure 3.10: First Aloha Week Court 1947
Source: Hawaii State Archives, Date: 1947

In addition to publicity from Pan American's flights across the Pacific, interest in traveling to the South Pacific was stirred by James Michener's book, *Tales of the South Pacific*, published in 1947 (Michener 1947). Stories from the book were adopted into a Broadway musical, *South Pacific*, by Rodgers and Hammerstein in 1949 (Broadway Musical Home 2020). In 1953, Hollywood also glamorized characters in WWII with the film, *From Here to Eternity*, with the famous kiss on the beach scene in Hawaii (Brogdon 1953). This was followed by the movie, *South Pacific*, in 1958. The American public as well as other parts of the world were being enticed to travel to Hawaii and the South Pacific as exotic, romantic destinations. With pent up demand to travel and more people familiar with the islands, travel to Hawaii boomed. Visitors to Hawaii increased from 15,000 in 1946 to 171,400 in 1958 (Hawaii Tourism Authority 2020).

Numerous entrepreneurs responded to the increases in tourists by developing hotels, tour companies, and transportation companies during the 1950s. Roy Kelley built the Islander Hotel in 1947, followed by the Edgewater hotel in 1951 and the Reef Hotel in 1955. Kelley's belief was that tourists would want affordable accommodations and built an empire consisting of affordable hotels before subsequent generations expanded into luxury hotels (McDermott 1990, chap. 3). Matson continued its investments into luxury hotels by building the Surfrider Hotel next to the Moana in 1952 and the Princess Kaiulani Hotel in 1955 (Hawaii Hotel Association 1990). Henry J. Kaiser built the Hawaiian Village Hotel in 1954. Other hotels built in Waikiki during this period were the Waikiki Biltmore Hotel and the Waikikian Hotel designed by George J. "Pete" Wimberly (Wimberly, Allison, Tong & Goo 2015).

On the Neighbor islands, Inter-Island Resorts was formed from the breakup of Inter-Island Steam Navigation Company into four separate companies in 1950. At the time, Inter-Island Resorts owned only the Kona Inn and Kauai Inn. In later decades, Inter-Island Resorts, through subsequent expansion, became Hawaii's largest Neighbor Island hotel chain (Allen 2004, 78–84).

Lyle Guslander in 1954 purchased and renamed a hotel on Kauai, The Coco Palms. Guslander hired Grace Buscher to manage the hotel. She infused the Hawaiian culture throughout the hotel and created a tropical paradise with its coconut palms, fishponds, lagoons, and torch lighting ceremony that tourists envisioned that they would experience in Hawaii. The success of the Coco Palms was followed by purchases of the Maui Palms and Kona Palms. These hotels formed the basis for the formation of Island Holidays as the second major inter-island hotel chain (Allen 2004, 84–90).

Future development of the Neighbor Islands was being contemplated by other companies. The Pioneer Mill was owned by Amfac, Inc. formerly known as American Factors, which started in the retail and sugar business. American Factors was known as one of the *Big Five* companies in Hawaii and had extensive land holdings (Encyclopedia.com 2021). The Board of Pioneer Mill voted in 1956 to proceed in developing Kaanapali on Maui as a "second Waikiki". In 1957, Matson bought 1,500 acres at Wailea for future development. These two decisions would begin the era of master planned resorts in Hawaii (Center for Tourism Policy Studies 1994). Most tourism planning up to this point in time was being done by the private sector and not the government.

The 1950s also saw the beginnings of tour companies and the introduction of tour buses capable of transporting large numbers of tourists around the island. Little information has been documented about tour companies in Hawaii because the tour companies are a part of the tourism industry that works mostly behind the scenes in wholesaling tour packages through travel agents. Similarly, the activities of ground transportation companies that provided sightseeing tours also were not documented well even though the companies were regulated by the government. Robert Allen provides a description of the early days of tour companies in Hawaii through his personal experiences as manager of Grey Line Hawaii beginning in 1949 (Allen 2004, 113–22).

Grey Line was a national transportation company with extensive contacts including travel agents, hotels and airlines that could promote travel to Hawaii. The national efforts were effective in fostering Grey Line Hawaii's growth as one of the major sightseeing companies in the islands. In the early years, sightseeing usually was done by limousines carrying nine to twelve passengers. Grey Line was the first to bring sightseeing buses to Hawaii that could accommodate forty-five passengers. The bus passenger capacity coincided with the standard seating of forty-four passengers for a DC-4. In 1952, the first large, organized tour group arrived in Hawaii with 150 participants staying at the Edgewater Hotel (McDermott 1990, 62–65). This was an early sign of future changes when travel would be transformed from "class to mass". Given the limited capacity of airplanes, the explosive growth in group inclusive travel to Hawaii was still yet to come two decades later.

Up to now, not much has been said about organized efforts to promote travel to Hawaii except mentioning the publishing of *Paradise of the Pacific* in 1888 to promote Hawaii to the world and establishment of the Hawaii Promotion Bureau in 1903. Promotion plays an important role in disseminating information about a destination to attract tourists. The Bureau printed brochures and pamphlets to distribute to potential visitors through steamship and railway agencies. It also placed advertisements in leading mainland periodicals. About half of the initial funding for the Bureau came from the Territorial Government and the other half from private sources. The Bureau's name was changed to the Hawaii Tourist Bureau in 1919 and continued to participate in promotional efforts throughout the years. After the Second World War (WWII), the Bureau's name was changed to the Hawaii Visitors Bureau (Hawaii Visitors & Convention Bureau 2020). A more detailed discussion of government efforts to promote Hawaii's tourism is deferred until Chapter 7.

Private sector efforts to promote tourism to Hawaii probably exceeded that of the government, since businesses had more resources available for advertising their services as part of a trip to Hawaii. The tourist-related promotion by Matson Navigation Company would be one example to lure passengers through destination advertising which could be distributed directly through its own companies and indirectly through its network of suppliers and affiliates. The efforts of Pan American Airlines across the Pacific brought widespread attention to Hawaii as a glamourous, exotic destination. United Airlines also supported the dissemination of tourist brochures on Hawaii as can be seen below in a photo of United Airlines counter agents with a Hawaii promotion brochure in Washington, D.C.

Figure 3.11: United Airlines counter agents with Hawaii promotion brochure. Source: Hawaii State Archives, Date: ca. 1953; Photographer: Ankers, Del

In addition to the efforts of the transportation companies, attention to the Hawaiian Islands was brought about by complimentary activities of individuals and the private sector. Duke Kahanamoku winning Olympic Gold medals in 1912 and 1920 brought world-wide attention to Hawaii. Duke, furthermore, popularized surfing and is considered to be the father of modern surfing (SurferToday.com 2020). Disney's production in 1937 of an animated cartoon called *Hawaiian Holiday* included feeble attempts at surfing by one of the characters (Disney 2020).

Figure 3.12: The Hawaiian Room of the Lexington Hotel in New York City
Source: Courtesy of the Hula Preservation Society

The Hawaiian Room at the Lexington Hotel in New York City popularized Hawaiian culture by bringing the best singers, dancers, and musicians from Hawaii. As described by Keau George, Collections Manager for the Hula Preservation Society, the Aloha Maids in the picture above "*were the first line of hula dancers to perform in the Hawaiian Room of the Lexington Hotel in New York City. They are pictured here, circa 1938, with the Ray Kinney Orchestra. The three hula dancers dressed in ti-leaf skirts kneel while performing with Hawaiian feathered rattles (ʻuliʻuli). Mr. Kinney stands behind them center stage leading the 10-member band, including piano, ukulele, guitar, clarinet, trumpet, standing bass, and drum musicians.*" (George 2021).

On the U.S. mainland, Donn Beach opened a chain of restaurants during the 1930s and 1940s called Don the Beachcomber, creating a fantasized South Pacific motif including a bamboo Tiki Bar with fishing nets draped on the walls and a rum cocktail called the Mai Tai (Geary 2016). He moved to Hawaii after the war and created the Waikiki Village in 1956, which was the forerunner of the International Marketplace (Centers 2020).

One of the most successful and longest enduring promotional activities was a radio show called *Hawaii Calls*. The show was conceived and narrated by Webley Edwards. The show was broadcast every Saturday from the Moana Hotel. Each show opened with the sound of waves at Waikiki Beach and featured live Hawaiian music (Rossetti 2020). The first show was broadcast on July 3, 1935, just four months before Pan American's inaugural flight from San Francisco to Honolulu on November 22, 1935. The show continued broadcasting until 1975. At its peak, *Hawaii Calls* was broadcast to over 750 radio stations throughout the world. Nothing could compare to its effectiveness in reaching so many potential visitors every week for four decades. The picture shows Al Kealoha Perry's troupe of eleven musicians and entertainers who performed on *Hawaii Calls* in 1937.

Figure 3.13: Al Kealoha Perry's Hawaii Calls Musicians 1937
Source: Hawaii State Archives, Date: ca. 1937; Photographer: Luke's Photo Studio

Hawaii Calls made many Hawaiian performers famous throughout the U.S. and the world. Alfred Apaka, known as the "Golden Voice of Hawaii", performed on Hawaii Calls during the 1940s and then extended the popularity of Hawaiian music through other radio and television broadcasts during the 1950s (Thielges 2020).

Figure 3.14: Hula dancers, Kodak Hula Show, Waikiki
Source: Hawaii State Archives, Date: 1937-1941; Photographer: Crabb, Roy F., d. 1966 / Kodak Hawaii

Another popular show was the Kodak Hula Show held in Waikiki that entertained visitors for sixty-five years (Hawaii History.org 2020). The vice-president and manager of Kodak Hawaii wanted to promote picture taking by providing a free hula show during the day. The picture shows hula dancers and musicians in the Kodak Hula Show across the beach in Waikiki during the early years of the show.

By 1958, the West Coast of the United States was the major tourist market to Hawaii. Tourists came on the luxurious Matson *White Ships* or by first-class air. Honolulu was the main destination. Tourists could fly to the Neighbor Islands on one of the inter-island airlines. The number of hotel rooms quadrupled from 1,038 in 1947 to 4,025 in 1958. Hotel rooms on the Neighbor Islands doubled from 566 in 1947 to 1,040 in 1958. Visitor expenditures increased over ten times, from $6.3 million in 1946 to $82.7 million in 1958 (Hawaii Visitors Bureau 1964, 15,40). In the Winter

1958 edition of *Business Horizons*, an article by Thomas Hitch, "Hawaii-Island Paradise with Economic Potential," stated: "*The American Society of Travel Agents knows that, next to Europe. more people think of Hawaii as their 'dream vacation' destination than any other place in the world*" (Hitch 1958, 85).

Summary

Tourism to Hawaii began with humble beginnings with fur traders stopping off to replenish supplies on their way to Canton, China. As the fur trade declined, the crews of whaling ships replaced them in large numbers, which encouraged the construction of rudimentary boarding facilities. These were the early tourists to the islands during the period of sailing ships. Given the long and uncomfortable trip, most passengers coming to Hawaii probably came out of necessity for business or other purposes other than vacationing in the islands.

Tourists for leisure and recreation would not be seen in large numbers until the era of steamships traveling at faster speeds and with comfortable facilities for passengers. During the early 1900s, ships constructed as passenger-freight combinations were designed with mostly first-class cabins to meet the needs of high-income travelers who had the time and means to vacation in Hawaii. The introduction of all-passenger ships in the late 1920s and 1930s was still designed with serving the needs of high-income travelers, and some were refitted in later years to only first- class cabins. Traveling on the Matson *White Ships* to Hawaii was luxurious. Docking at Aloha Tower in Honolulu Harbor was a festive Boat Day with the Royal Hawaiian Band playing, hula dancers, flower lei dropped across the waters, and young men diving for coins thrown by passengers into the water.

The era of the China Clippers flying to the Far East and South Pacific via Honolulu brought only a small number of tourists because of the limited passenger capacity on the flying airboats. The flights were luxurious with a lounge, dining room and sleeping berths to make it comfortable for first-class passengers on the 16 to 18-hour flight to Hawaii from the West Coast. Tourists on the China Clippers still were higher income persons traveling to and/or beyond Hawaii. The advent of larger, faster airplanes capable of carrying more passengers after WWII was the beginning of travel to Hawaii becoming more affordable. Travel to Hawaii increased more than a hundred-fold after the war up until statehood.

The pre-statehood period can be considered the introduction and early growth periods of tourism in Hawaii. Several patterns of growth emerged during this period, which remained applicable throughout successive time periods. Transportation was one of the most critical factors underlying tourism growth. Improvements in speed, comfort, convenience, and decreases in fares made travel to Hawaii available to a wider segment of the population. Tourist facilities in Hawaii were developed in response to the types of travelers arriving, initially boarding houses and crude hotels and later first-class hotels. Transportation companies often were one of the first to develop lodging and tourist-related facilities to attract people to travel with them and accommodate the needs of their passengers.

Government involvement encompassed subsidies for transportation development for both steamship and air travel. Tourist facilities were subsidized as exemplified in the Hawaiian Government financing the construction of the Hawaiian Hotel.

The purpose of this subsidy was to create new jobs and additional income for the residents of the islands. Government involvement also took the form of regulation as in the case of the CAB, which controlled the entry of new airlines into the U.S. airline industry and entry into airline routes. Government provided funds for promoting Hawaii to potential travelers with the establishment of the Hawaii Promotion Bureau, which evolved into the Hawaii Visitors Bureau after WWII. These efforts supplemented the promotional activities of the private sector.

The transportation and hotel companies funded activities to entice tourists to the Hawaiian Islands through advertising of their services within the context of Hawaii as an exotic island paradise. The glory days of Matson's *White Ships* and Pan American's adventures across the Pacific brought attention to Hawaii, the Far East, and the South Pacific. Publicity from early writers such as Mark Twain and later James Michener incited dreams about visiting the South Pacific. Disney, Broadway, and Hollywood brought these dreams to life through their music and movies. The major source of tourists was the West Coast of the U.S. mainland.

The treaty to lease Pearl Harbor in 1887 recognized the strategic importance of Hawaii for the U.S. military. The influence of the U.S. military and wars upon travel to Hawaii began with the Spanish-American War fought in the Philippines. WWI did not have much impact upon travel to Hawaii, but WWII brought thousands of military and civilian personnel to the islands. The bombing of Pearl Harbor made an indelible memory on the minds of Americans. The Korean War had a similar effect to WWII but to a lesser degree.

A last note before continuing to the next chapter, investment in transportation and tourist facilities involved high risk and often resulted in financial losses. The Hawaiian Hotel suffered losses for years as reflected in the turnover of management companies. Overcapacity in hotel rooms resulted in bankruptcies. Ships were able to adapt by first offering limited passenger capacity and then constructing passenger-freight combinations, still relying upon cargo as the main source of revenues. The early airline industry experienced crashes and intense competition resulting in operating losses. The introduction and early growth stages of Hawaii were fraught with difficulties, uneven performance, and high risk of failure. These same challenges continued throughout subsequent stages of Hawaii's tourism life cycle.

Chapter 4
Growth Stage:
Golden Age of Jet Travel & Mass Travel

Overview

By the time that Hawaii became the 50th State of the United States, Hawaii already was known throughout the world through weekly broadcasts of Hawaii Calls; movies with major Hollywood stars including Esther Williams, Bing Crosby, and Burt Lancaster; Hawaiian singers, dancers and musicians who performed throughout the world; and Hawaiian personalities such as Duke Kahanamoku and Alfred Apaka. Ties to the United States were strengthened further by Hawaii's role in WWII and its strategic role in the Pacific for the military. Americans already were flocking to Hawaii as their dream vacation destination. Statehood in 1959 was the final step in securing the fate of Hawaii with the United States. Statehood provided confidence for investors and businesses to increase their activities in the State. American tourists were attracted by an exotic, island paradise within the safe boundaries of the United States.

The 1950s and 1960s were known as the Golden Age of Air Travel. Airplanes were spacious with lounges for passengers, gourmet meals were served on board, and glamourous flight attendants provided first-class services for passengers.

Passengers dressed semi-formal with men in suits/sport coats and women in fancy dresses as if they were celebrating a special occasion (Design You Trust 2020, 1–2). The early jets extended the glamour of flying with on-board services and amenities as well as airport lounges for first-class passengers.

Under CAB regulations, airlines were not allowed to compete in terms of price, and competition was in terms of the services and amenities provided for passengers. The Golden Age of Jet Travel accelerated the growth of tourism in Hawaii as jet travel reduced travel time across the continents and oceans, and airlines continued their expansion across the Pacific to Asia, Oceania, and Hawaii. Larger aircraft and changes in CAB regulations that facilitated inexpensive group travel brought about The Age of Mass Travel to Hawaii.

Golden Age of Jet Travel 1959–1969

Hawaii became a state on August 21, 1959, and less than a month later, Pan American introduced all jet airline service through Honolulu on September 14, 1959. Using Boeing 707 aircraft, the flight time from the West Coast was reduced to about five hours and up to 180 passengers could be carried (Hawaii Aviation 2015a). There was high interest in traveling to Hawaii. James Michener published his book, *Hawaii*, which later was made into a movie (Michener 1959). The television series, *Adventures in Paradise*, based on Michener's *Tales of the South Pacific*, was broadcast from 1959–1963 (Webmaster 2020a). A detective series, *Hawaiian Eye*, was televised from 1959–1963 (Webmaster 2020b). The iconic television series, *Hawaii Five-0*, began in 1968 and ended in 1980 ("The Hawaii Five-O Home Page" 2020). *Hawaii Five-0*, with twelve seasons, was one of the most popular and longest running television series. To Americans, Hawaii portrayed the image of the South Pacific.

Airlines were complaining in 1959 that they had to turn away business due to the lack of hotel rooms in Hawaii. Concerned over the growing shortage of visitor accommodations, the Hawaii State Planning Office was directed to undertake a study, *Visitor Destination Areas in Hawaii* (Hawaii State Planning Office 1960). One of the major motivating factors was to improve the economy of the neighbor islands. The study completed in 1960 recommended a program for public improvements to accelerate the growth of tourism through the construction of tourist facilities, especially on the neighbor islands. The study is discussed in Chapter 7 on Tourism Planning and Promotion.

Hawaii's prominence was kept at the forefront in the minds of consumers throughout the 1960s. Royalty including the King of Jordan, King of Thailand and the Crown Prince of Japan with his wife, Princess Michiko, visited the islands. Dignitaries including the President of Finland and every president of the United States from President Eisenhower to President Nixon came to Hawaii (Hawaii Aviation 2015b). The United States Space Program was at its peak racing to the moon. From 1962, with the Project Mercury astronauts to the moon landing astronauts of Apollo 11 and 12 in 1969, every spacecraft and astronauts landing in the Pacific Ocean were transported to Hickam Air Force Base. The picture shows the arrival ceremony in 1960 for President Eisenhower at Honolulu International Airport with Governor Quinn and military personnel.

Figure 4.1: President Dwight D. Eisenhower at Honolulu International Airport
Source: Hawaii State Archives, Date: 1960, Photographer: Honolulu Star-Bulletin.

Hollywood continued its love for Hawaii with a trilogy of movies starring Elvis Presley. The first movie in 1961, *Blue Hawaii*, was Elvis' largest commercial success with fourteen songs, and the soundtrack album being number one on the Billboard pop charts for twenty weeks (Graceland 2020). One of the most memorable scenes was Elvis singing the Hawaiian Wedding Song on the grounds of the Coco Palms Hotel. Elvis' second movie, *Girls, Girls, Girls*, opened in 1962, and *Paradise Hawaiian Style* opened in 1966 (Elvis Australia 2020). With the popularity of Elvis, an entire new generation of younger people would now dream of vacationing in Hawaii. In addition, the movie, *Hawaii*, based on Michener's novel opened in 1966 starring Charlton Heston (Canby 1966).

With the publicity from the visits of dignitaries, astronauts, Hollywood movies, television programs and Hawaii Calls, the American public as well as people living in other parts of the world were being lured constantly to visit Hawaii. Domestic and international airlines increased their services to and through Hawaii. By 1963, there were eight major overseas airlines with scheduled flights to Hawaii: British Overseas Airways Corp., Canadian Pacific Air Lines, Japan Air Lines, Northwest Airlines, Pan American World Airways, Philippine Air Lines, Qantas Empire Airways and United Air Lines. Direct flights were coming from Australia, Canada, Japan, and the Philippines. In addition, British Overseas Airways was flying from London to Sydney via Hawaii (Hawaii Aviation 2015b). Aloha Airlines and Hawaiian Airlines provided the inter-island flights.

Hotel developers responded to the expected increases in visitors with the opening of new luxury hotels. On Oahu, the Kahala Hilton Hotel opened on beachfront property near the Waialae Country Club Golf Course outside of Waikiki. The hotel was the first major hotel to be located outside of the main tourist area, Waikiki. The picture of The Kahala Hotel shows the hotel towering over its beachfront lagoon with mountains in the background. There were doubts whether the hotel would succeed.

Figure 4.2: The Kahala Hotel
Source: Courtesy of The Kahala Hotel

The hotel developer was astute in signing a contract with Hilton International Hotels to manage the hotel. Hilton International was the world's first international hotel chain with a world-wide client base (The Kahala Hotel & Resort 2020). From 1963–1965, Robert H. Burns was a project coordinator at the hotel. Burns became the general manager of the hotel in 1965. The hotel's design and services introduced standards of luxury never before seen in the islands. The hotel became an icon for both visitors and residents (World Biographical Encyclopedia 2020). Burns in 1970 formed his own successful, luxury hotel company, Regent International Hotels based in Hong Kong (Regent Hotels 2020). Hilton Corporation no longer manages the hotel, and it is now known as *The Kahala Hotel*.

The second luxury hotel on Oahu was the Ilikai Hotel which opened a month after the Kahala Hilton (Napier 2014). The State of Hawaii was the first state in the United States to adopt a

Condominium Law which allowed for fee simple ownership of individual units located within a multi-unit structure (Ducharme 2020). The Ilikai was first intended to be a residential complex, and rooms were large since they were designed as apartments. The initial project encountered difficulties. The project was redesigned to be a hotel and condominium complex by Chinn Ho, who was one of the initial investors and a well-known financier in Hawaii.

The Ilikai Hotel was the first luxury high rise in Waikiki with twenty-six stories and three wings shaped in a Y. It opened with 1,000 rooms with half as hotel rooms and half as condominiums. The hotel was the first hotel-condominium combination in the islands as well as the first condotel in the United States. Condominium owners could use their units as their residences or as vacation rentals that the hotel would include in its room inventory. The sale of the condominiums brought cash immediately back to investors, which lowered the risk of developing the project. The picture of the Ilikai Hotel shows the hotel at its opening.

Figure 4.3: Ilikai Hotel at its opening
Source: Courtesy of the Ilikai Hotel

Even with the openings of the Kahala Hilton and Ilikai Hotel, overbooking occurred in 1965 when some visitors were turned away by hotels and housed at the YMCA. Other hotel projects on Oahu included the construction of the Outrigger Hotel, a new wing of the Surfrider Hotel on the west side of the Moana Hotel, and additions to the Reef Hotel. The Hilton Hawaiian Village had extensive plans to expand their facilities with a new Rainbow Tower, Mid-Pacific Conference Center and Coral Ballroom. Amfac and United Airlines partnered to build the 500-room Waikiki Beachcomber Hotel.

Chinn Ho extended his investment in the hotel industry by building the Makaha Inn and Country Club (Hawaii Hotel Association 1990). The hotel was the first major resort hotel to be developed on the North Shore of Oahu far from Waikiki. The strategy was to take advantage of Makaha Beach's reputation for the annual World Surfing Championship competition. Thousands of tourists came to see the big-wave competition as well as organizers, media personnel and participants with their family and friends.

Expansion of hotels on the Neighbor Islands began in 1960 with the opening of the Kauai Surf as the first Neighbor Island destination resort. Lyle Guslander opened the King Kamehameha Hotel in Kona on the Big Island as part of the Island Holidays hotel chain, which included the Coco Palms, Maui Palms and Kona Palms (Allen 2004, 84–90). Matson announced a fourteen-year development plan for land which it owned in Wailea on Maui (Wailea Resort Association 2020). The first master planned resort area at Kaanapali, Maui opened in 1962 with the Royal Lahaina Beach Club followed by the Sheraton Maui in 1963. The Sheraton Maui was the first Neighbor Island resort hotel to be owned by a national hotel chain (Russo 2013). The Bishop estate announced plans for a 1,100-acre resort at Keauhou-Kona (Gomes 1999).

In 1965, RockResorts developed and managed the 154–room Mauna Kea Beach Resort on the Kohala Coast of the Big Island. RockResorts was created in 1956 by Laurance Rockefeller, who was known for developing luxury resort hotels in spectacular natural environments. The design of the Mauna Kea Beach Hotel, its furnishings and extensive art collection created an elegant atmosphere for a secluded hideaway overlooking the turquoise waters of Kaunaoa Bay. At the time, the hotel was the most expensive hotel ever built and considered one of the greatest hotels in the world. Rockefeller wanted to maintain the serenity of the beautiful natural scenery. For thirty years, televisions were not provided in the rooms (Services 2020; RockResorts 2020). Following Rockefeller's investment, additional development of the Big Island's "Gold Coast" was being proposed.

Amidst the expansion of hotels, there also were turnovers in ownership and management of hotels. In 1959, Matson Navigation Company decided to concentrate on shipping and sold its hotels to Sheraton Corporation (Matson 2020, 6). Henry J. Kaiser in 1961 sold his half interest in the Hawaiian Village to Hilton Hotels which renamed the hotel Hilton Hawaiian Village (Hilton Hawaiian Village 2020). In 1964, Hilton Hotels separated into Hilton International Hotels, which managed only international properties and Hilton Hotels which only managed properties in the United States (Maffei 2018). The Kahala Hilton remained under Hilton International Hotels and the Hawaiian Village was kept under Hilton Hotels management. This was a unique situation for Hilton International and Hilton Hotels to manage properties in the same location. In 1969, Lyle Guslander sold Island Holidays Hotels and Island Holidays Tours to Amfac.

The 1960s also saw the entry of foreign investors in the Hawaii hotel industry. Kenji Osano first opened a restaurant called Kyo-Ya in 1956 on Kalakaua Avenue. In 1960, Osano formed Kyo-Ya Ltd. as a subsidiary of Japan-based Kokusai Kogyo. Kyo-Ya Ltd. purchased the Princess Kaiulani and Moana-Surfrider Hotels from Sheraton Hotel Corporation in 1961 (Lynch 1996). This was only the beginning of Kyo-Ya's investment in Hawaii Hotels. Kyo-Ya was followed by other Japanese companies purchasing or building hotels throughout the islands. The boom in Japanese investments in Hawaii still was yet to come in subsequent decades.

Canadian investors opened the ten-unit Hale Napili and sixteen-unit Napili Beach Club on Maui. This was the beginning of Canadian investments on Maui, constructing resort condominiums especially in Kihei (Sakata 1977). Canadians preferred staying in condominiums, because they stayed for several weeks to over a month to escape the long harsh winters in Canada. Condominiums provided an economical way of vacationing in Hawaii, since they could prepare their own meals and do their household chores less expensively than staying in a hotel. In addition, larger condominium units could accommodate more people than the average hotel room. The large condominium units were ideal for families or friends willing to stay together to share expenses.

The tropical weather, white sand beaches and beautiful natural scenery were always among the main attractions for visiting Hawaii. Vacationing in Hawaii was enhanced by the opening of historic sites and tourist attractions such as the USS Arizona Memorial, City of Refuge as a National Park at Honaunau on the Big Island of Hawaii, Polynesian Cultural Center in Laie, Ulu Mau Village at Ala Moana Beach Park, Sea Life Park at Waimanalo, and Paradise Bird Park in Manoa Valley. In the evening, tourists could listen to Don Ho singing *Tiny Bubbles* at Dukes in the International Marketplace, Kui Lee singing his classic song *I'll Remember You* at the Barefoot Bar on the beach in Queens Surf

Restaurant as well as enjoy Polynesian Reviews with dancers and singers at major hotels or the Polynesian Cultural Center.

This time period also was a golden time for residents who enjoyed the beaches, historic sites, tourist attractions and local entertainers as much as the tourists. The historic sites and attractions were not only interesting places to experience but also educational. School children would have excursions to visit the historic sites and attractions. Residents could purchase one-time passes at discounted kamaaina rates or annual passes to the tourist attractions available only to residents. Residents also went to see Don Ho to *suck um up* and listen to Kui Lee's haunting singing of *I'll Remember You.* The luxury hotels provided dining, entertainment, and banquet facilities for residents to celebrate special occasions. Wedding receptions and events were held in hotel ballrooms.

Waikiki was not crowded with high rises. Kalakaua Avenue, the main street running through Waikiki, was lined with small shops and restaurants patronized by residents. Beach access was not blocked by massive hotels or shopping complexes. Residents could enjoy a day swimming, surfing, sunbathing, and/or picnicking at the beaches in Waikiki. One could hope to catch a glimpse of a movie star or celebrity riding in a canoe paddled by beachboys, taking surfing lessons, sipping a mai tai or dining beachside.

Not all that was happening during this time was fun and enjoyment. The United States started sending combat troops to Vietnam starting in 1965 (Taylor 2015). Like previous wars fought in Asia or the Pacific, military and civilian personnel associated with the war effort transited or were stationed in Hawaii. During their one-year tour of duty in Vietnam, troops were allowed a week of rest and recuperation (R&R) outside of Vietnam. R&R destinations included Hawaii, Australia, Japan, Thailand, and several other Asian countries. Hawaii was the destination for family men, newlyweds, and sweethearts (Chandler 2018). Troops would come to Hawaii to meet their family or friends coming from the U.S. mainland. They could stay with their wives or girlfriends at the Army's Fort DeRussy R&R Center on Waikiki Beach. The number of R&R visitors to Hawaii reached a peak of 246,000 in 1969, accounting for 18 percent of all visitors to the islands (Hawaii Visitors Bureau 1964, no. 1970). The popularity of Hawaii as a R&R destination stirred plans to build a hotel at Fort DeRussy.

Expansion of air services to the islands occurred through the growth of nonscheduled airlines. In addition to scheduled airlines such as Pan American and United Airlines, there were numerous non-scheduled air carriers that were chartered by organizations for their sole use. Using charter airlines resulted in lower fares due to lower costs of operations. The charter airlines were operating through a loophole in CAB regulations which did not cover irregular, nonscheduled flight operations. In 1962, the CAB provided certification for nonscheduled airlines which met its requirements (Harvard Law Review 1963, 1450–52). The charter airlines were providing services for Affinity Charters and Travel Group Charters to respective destinations.

In 1966, the CAB granted indirect air carrier authority to tour operators to charter an aircraft to conduct an Inclusive Tour Charter (ITC) (U.S.C. H.I. and F. Commerce 1968, 128). The ITC was a roundtrip tour which combined air transportation and land services. The tour must be for at least seven days and provide overnight accommodations for a minimum of three places, other than the place of origin, fifty air miles apart. The ITC was commonly known as the Three-Stop Inclusive Tour Charter (Choy 1978, 69). Tourists to Hawaii on ITCs would land in Honolulu, tour the island of Oahu, and then visit at least two neighbor islands to meet the three-stop minimum requirement.

In the first full year of operating ITCs, 175 tours were approved, carrying approximately 30,000 passengers in 1967. It was estimated that of the total ITC passengers, 25,000 traveled on tours to Hawaii. The CAB approved 800 ITC tours to be operated between the U.S. mainland to Hawaii for 1968 and estimated that tour passengers would increase to 136,000 (U.S.C.H.I. and F. Commerce 1968, 128). The ITC tours created a large market for economy vacations that middle income Americans could afford to purchase to visit Hawaii. Scheduled airfares for point-to-point travel still were expensive, and higher income individuals were typically the ones traveling on scheduled flights. The success of the ITCs to Hawaii was the beginning of the transformation from *class to mass tourism* for Hawaii.

With increased demand for travel to Hawaii, scheduled airlines were requesting to operate new routes to Hawaii. The CAB in 1965 opened the Trans-Pacific Route Case, which took three years to settle (Keyes 1968). In 1968 existing carriers, Northwest, Pan American and United Airlines were awarded additional routes to Hawaii. Five new carriers, American, Braniff, Continental, Trans-World and Western Airlines were awarded route authority to Hawaii (Hawaii Aviation 2015b). One of the conditions for the routes was that the new airlines would have to provide direct flights from the U.S. mainland to Hilo in addition to their direct flights to Honolulu. The jet airport at Hilo was completed in 1965 as part of the State's plan to have two entry points into the islands. The plan was to have a two-way flow of visitors through the islands. Visitors landing in Honolulu traveling to the Neighbor Islands could depart from Hilo to return to the mainland. Visitors landing in Hilo could return to the mainland from Honolulu.

Around the same time, the CAB was in process of approving a common fare package for the scheduled airlines which would allow visits to four islands at an additional fare of $5 for each intermediate leg to visit an island and a free turn-around leg (United States. Civil Aeronautics Board 1979). The ITCs, direct flights to Hilo and common fare package made visits to the neighbor islands attractive by providing inexpensive tour packages and minimal airfare to visit the Neighbor Islands for thousands of visitors, who otherwise may have visited only Honolulu and/or one to two islands.

The Age of Mass Travel to Hawaii 1970–1979

Although the introduction of jets resulted in more people traveling to Hawaii, passengers on scheduled flights were primarily free independent travelers (FIT) until the introduction of ITCs which fostered inexpensive group travel. The capacity of commercial jet aircrafts was limited to 150–200 passengers. The introduction of wide-bodied jets increased passenger capacities. The Boeing-747 airplane had a passenger capacity of 334–490 passengers (Boeing 2021). The DC-10 and L-1011 airplanes had passenger capacities of 250. The Boeing-747 eventually became the dominant wide-bodied jet due to problems with the DC-10 and L-1011. The introduction of the wide-bodied jets initially emphasized comfort and luxury. The wide-bodied jets provided more comfortable seating with extensive in-flight services including meals and drinks. First-class passengers on the Boeing-747 had a lounge to enjoy cocktails on the upper deck. Because the CAB still did not allow open price competition, airlines continued to compete on non-price attributes such as in-flight services and the convenience of flight schedules.

Honolulu Airport had to construct special jetways to accommodate the large jumbo jets. Pan American's Boeing-747 flights to Honolulu started in March 1970. Jumbo jets began landing at General Lyman Field in Hilo in 1971. Although the jumbo jets could accommodate large groups, airlines did not book Group Inclusive Tours (GIT) groups on scheduled flights until the CAB reduced the minimum number of passengers necessary for inclusive tours (Board 1970, 434–66). Initially, tour wholesalers had to fill a minimum of 154 seats per contracted flight series. In 1975, CAB approval of One-Stop Inclusive Tours (OTC) eliminated the minimum three stops required for ITCs resulting in even lower prices for a vacation in Hawaii (Choy 1978, 69; Grimes 1975). The minimum number of seats for an inclusive tour was reduced to 40 and then 20, making it easier for tour wholesalers to organize groups. Scheduled airlines introduced GIT fares to fill the seats on their jumbo jets. The OTC, jumbo jets and GIT fares opened the floodgates for middle income America to enjoy affordable vacations in Hawaii.

By 1976, visitors traveling as part of a group comprised almost forty percent of total visitors to Hawaii. The peak volume of group travel to Hawaii was reached in 1978 with group visitors accounting for 1.12 million of the total 3.68 million visitors to Hawaii (Hawaii Visitors Bureau 1964, no. 1980). The transformation from *class to mass tourism* to Hawaii was completed within a relatively short time of ten years since the approval of ITCs.

The term *mass travel* often has negative connotations, with visions of hordes of tourists descending upon a destination and inundating the residents and physical facilities. On the other hand, mass travel reflects the democratization of travel for all income levels to afford vacations that previously only the wealthy could enjoy. The balance between the positive and negative impacts of tourism upon Hawaii are discussed in Chapter 9.

Regarding hotel development during this time, the Ala Moana Hotel opened on Oahu in 1970 with over 1,100 rooms (Hawaii Hotel Association 1990, I and II:94). The hotel was connected to Ala Moana Center by a pedestrian ramp. Ala Moana Shopping Center was the largest open-air shopping center in the United States. The Center was located only a few minutes' drive or bus ride from Waikiki and was walking distance from the Ilikai Hotel. Sheraton Corporation anticipated the increase in group travel and built the 32–story, 1,700–room Sheraton Waikiki Hotel on the beach next to the Royal Hawaiian Hotel. To maximize the number of ocean-view rooms, which commanded higher rates, the hotel was built in a V-shape. The second floor above the lobby had a large ballroom and meetings rooms for handling groups of various sizes. When it opened in 1971, the Sheraton Waikiki was one of the largest resort hotels in the world. The

416–room Hale Koa Hotel, initially conceived to serve R&R visits, opened four years later beachside at Fort DeRussy. The Hale Koa Hotel provided accommodations for military personnel and qualified civilian personnel on vacation or business trips to Hawaii (Hale Koa Hotel 2020).

Another major project for Waikiki was Chris Hemmeter's plans for the Hyatt Regency Waikiki as part of the Hemmeter Center Complex, which included seventy shops, several restaurants and meeting rooms for conventions. The hotel was designed with twin towers, forty stories high with a total of 1,234 rooms (Hawaii Business 1977b, 19–22). A few blocks away, towards the Ala Wai Canal, condominiums were being built for use as residences or vacation rentals. In 1976, the Waikiki Special Design District was established to limit future hotel construction in Waikiki (Schmidt, Peirson, and Lierman 2020). Plans to build hotels in Waikiki that were approved prior to 1976, however, were allowed to proceed. Outside of Waikiki, Del Webb Corporation of Las Vegas began construction of the Kuilima Hotel on the North Shore in expectation of gambling being approved by the State government (Hotel Online 2017).

Increased travel to the Neighbor Islands initiated further development of tourist-related facilities. The State wanted to encourage tourism development on the Neighbor Islands by providing the necessary infrastructure. The State built Keahole Airport in 1970 to serve both Kona and the South Kohala Coast on the island of Hawaii (Hawaii Aviation 2015c). The Queen Kaahumanu Highway was built in 1975. The highway stretched thirty-three miles along the Kona Coast, providing access to lands for future resort development. Over 3,000 acres of land was purchased in South Kohala for a master planned resort community. In Hilo, the Waiakea Village opened in 1972 and the Hilo Hawaiian Hotel opened in 1975. The Maui Intercontinental Hotel, Wailea Beach Hotel, and Kapalua Bay Hotels opened on Maui during the last half of the 1970s. (Hawaii Business 1977a, 32–36) The Neighbor Islands were beginning to create their separate identities from Oahu.

The large increase in group travel also fostered the growth of tour wholesale companies based in Hawaii. Tour wholesalers packaged the arrangements included in tours to Hawaii and sold the tour packages through retail travel agents. Ground transportation companies that provided tours around the islands, as well as the tourist attractions that were included in the tour packages, flourished. Trade Wind Tours became the largest of the tour wholesalers in Hawaii. Other companies included MacKenzie Travel, Hawaiian Holidays and Aloha Hawaii Travel (Fooks 1997, 3–4). Tour wholesalers in Hawaii had offices on the U.S. mainland to assist in the selling of their tours through retail travel agents and outbound tour wholesalers located on the mainland. Even though the distribution network for selling travel was becoming more complex, quantity discounts for tour arrangements achieved through large volumes of group travelers combined with lower group airfares continued to lower the costs of a vacation to Hawaii.

In regard to air transportation, one of the most important events of the decade was the deregulation of the U.S. airline industry. Congress passed the Airline Deregulation Act of 1978, which phased out the CAB and removed restrictions on fares and entry to routes (National Air & Space Museum 2020). U.S. airlines now could compete on fares and enter any route within the United States. Due to deregulation, thirteen airlines received approval for new routes between the U.S. mainland and Hawaii. The airlines were: American, Braniff, Continental, Delta, Eastern, Hawaiian, National, Ozark, Pacific Southwest, Trans-Caribbean Airways, Trans International, Western and World Airways. Pacific Southwest Airlines was one of the largest discount airlines (Hawaii Aviation 2015c). Trans International Airlines and World Airways were charter airlines.

The number of visitors to Hawaii continued to increase throughout the 1970s, despite the world-wide recession of 1974-1975 and Arab oil embargo by the Organization of Petroleum Exporting Countries (OPEC) that caused fuel shortages. The number of visitors increased to 2.2 million in 1972, 3.2 million in 1976, and 3.9 million in 1979. Of the total visitors, the number of international visitors more than doubled, from 472,265 in 1970 to 1,077,671 in 1979. International visitors accounted for more than one-fourth, 27 percent, of the total visitors in 1979 (Hawaii Visitors Bureau 1964, nos. 1970–1979).

The major international markets were Canada and Japan. Canadian visitors reached a peak of 311,710 visitors in 1978 and accounted for almost one-tenth, 8.5 percent, of all visitors. The number of Japanese visitors increased six-fold from 93,665 in 1970 to 577,490 in 1979, accounting for 14.5 percent of all visitors (Hawaii Visitors Bureau 1964, no. 1979). A substantial proportion of Canadian visitors went to Maui during their stay in Hawaii. Japanese visitors traveled in groups and tended to stay in Waikiki. Japanese visitors had the highest expenditures per day due to extensive shopping to bring back gifts for family, friends, and coworkers as their custom of *omiyage*.

Waikiki was transformed not only by the large high-rise hotels, but also by the large shopping centers and other commercial buildings built within the area. New shopping complexes included King's Alley, Hemmeter Center, Waikiki Shopping Plaza, and the Royal Hawaiian Shopping Center which was built in front of the Royal Hawaiian Hotel on Kalakaua Avenue (Hawaii Business 1977d, 68). The small shops and restaurants patronized by residents now were replaced by the shopping complexes, hotels, and commercial buildings. Large tour busses would pick up visitors from their hotels after breakfast for half-day or full-day tours around the island and return them to their hotels at noon or in the late afternoon. Evening tours also were available for sunset cruises, luaus, nightclub shows and evening tours to tourist attractions. Busloads of tourists would arrive late at night returning to their hotels after enjoying the show and dinner at the Polynesian Cultural Center.

Residents still would go to Waikiki for entertainment and dining; but the streets and sidewalks were crowded, group tourists would fill restaurants and nightclubs, the shopping complexes were targeting tourists, and there was limited public parking. Beach access was limited due to the construction of new hotels on the beach. Some hotels even corded off their beach frontage for exclusive use of their guests. Waikiki no longer was the playground for residents as it used to be during the Golden Years.

As might be expected from the growth in Japanese tourists, companies from Japan increased their investments in Hawaii

(U.S.C.S.C. on Commerce 1974, 19–20). Ohbayashi Gumi, one of Japan's largest construction companies bought the Sheraton Kauai. Tokyu Corporation, a major railroad company, was the company that bought 3,200 acres of land in South Kohala to develop the Mauna Lani planned resort community. Japanese investors purchased the Aloha Surf, Park Shore and Breakers Hotel which were smaller hotels in Waikiki. Seibu Group bought McInerny Department Stores and 1,000 acres in Makena, Maui. Sheraton Corporation decided to focus on managing hotels and sold the Sheraton Waikiki, Royal Hawaiian Hotel and Sheraton Maui Hotel to Kyo-Ya Ltd (Lynch 1996). Makaha Inn & Country Club was not performing as expected and was sold to Hawaii Daiichi Kanko.

Summary

The Golden Age of Jet Travel initiated the rapid growth of travel to Hawaii. The number of visitors increased at an annual average rate of growth of twenty-one percent per year. Visitor arrivals doubled every five years, reaching 1.5 million in 1969. The number of hotel rooms in Waikiki tripled from 5,286 in 1959 to 16,590 in 1969. The number of off-Waikiki hotel rooms increased to 1,859 with the openings of the Kahala Hilton and Makaha Inn & Country Club.

Even though there were more hotel rooms in Waikiki than on all the neighbor islands, the growth rate of hotel rooms on the neighbor islands exceeded that of Waikiki. The number of hotel rooms on the island of Hawaii grew fivefold to 3,166 in 1969; Maui almost tenfold to 2,743; and Kauai over tenfold to 2,565. The number of Westbound visitors who intended to visit Oahu and other islands increased to almost half a million by 1969. Each of the Neighbor Islands i.e., Hawaii, Maui and Kauai were receiving over 300,000 thousand visitors (Hawaii Visitors Bureau 1964, no. 1969).

Major changes in the tourism industry continued through the 1970s. The introduction of jumbo jets and inexpensive tour packages transformed travel to Hawaii from *class to mass* with GIT travelers comprising over one million of total visitors to the islands. The shift to mass travel also transformed Waikiki through construction of large high-rise hotels, shopping complexes and commercial buildings which replaced the small shops and restaurants patronized by residents. Waikiki now was catering primarily to tourists.

International visitors were becoming a more important market segment than in previous years. The growth in eastbound visitors from Asia exceeded that of westbound visitors. Japanese tourists were the largest international market, and they primarily traveled on group tours organized by Japanese wholesalers such as Japan Travel Bureau, Kintetsu, and Nippon Travel Agency. By the end of the 1970s, Japanese investors owned many of the luxury hotels in Waikiki as well as luxury hotels on Kauai and Maui. Japanese companies, moreover, were purchasing large acreage on the Neighbor Islands to develop master planned resort communities.

With limits placed on hotel construction in Waikiki, attention turned to development on the Neighbor Islands. The two resorts developed on the North Shore of Oahu were not successful. As mentioned earlier, Makaha Inn & Country Club was sold to Japanese investors. Gambling was not approved by the State government, and Kuilima Resort was doing so poorly that management was changed from Del Webb to Hyatt Hotels (Hawaii Business 1977c, 116). The Neighbor Islands offered better prospects with the opening of the first master planned resort in Kaanapali, which became the model for developing Wailea and resort communities on the South Kohala Coast. The State of Hawaii also had invested in airports and highways on the Neighbor Islands to facilitate economic development on each island.

The CAB requirement that ITCs had to have a minimum of three stops spurred travel to the Neighbor Islands. By 1979, over two million westbound visitors were traveling to the Neighbor Islands. The combined increase in the number of hotel rooms on the Neighbor Islands was almost equal to that of Oahu. From 1970-1979, hotel rooms on Oahu increased by 12,361 for a total of 33,967 hotel rooms for the island. Hotel rooms on the Neighbor Islands increased 11,305 for a total of 22,802 hotel rooms. Most of the increase for the Neighbor Islands was on Maui which accounted for one-fifth, 18.9 percent, of the total hotel rooms in the State. Waikiki still was the main destination area with over half, 54 percent, of all hotel rooms (Hawaii Visitors Bureau 1964, no. 1979).

The 1970s also saw hotel condominiums becoming a significant part of Hawaii's hotel industry. Of a total 9,690 hotel rooms on Maui, almost half, 47.8 percent, were condominiums. Condominiums comprised 28.7 percent of the total hotel rooms on Kauai. Condominiums were not a large part of the hotel inventories for Oahu or the island of Hawaii. The development of new resorts on the Neighbor Islands would continue as discussed in the next chapter.

Chapter 5

Mature Stage & Stagnation

Overview

The image of Hawaii was elevated throughout the 1960s by the visits of foreign dignitaries, U.S. presidents, and astronauts of the U.S. space program. Events in Hawaii were being reported through the news media throughout the world. Popular movies increased Hawaii's appeal to a younger generation, especially through Elvis Presley's romantic escapades in the islands. The demand to visit Hawaii was coming from not only the United States as the traditional market, but also from foreign countries.

The development of faster jet travel made it possible to penetrate markets farther away. For the United States, markets in the mid-west and east coast became within reasonable travel time due to the faster jets. Travelers from Asia, especially Japan, were visiting Hawaii in growing numbers. The introduction of jumbo jets lowered the cost of traveling overseas due to their larger passenger capacities which made it possible to offer lower fares. CAB approval of inclusive charters and group fares for both domestic and international routes made travel affordable to a larger segment of the world population.

Changes in aircraft technology coupled with CAB regulation of the airline industry continued to influence the type of travelers to Hawaii from the luxurious Golden Days of Jet Travel to GIT groups on jumbo jets. The total number of visitors to Hawaii increased sixteen-fold, from 242,994 in 1959 to 1,526,074 in 1969 to 3,966,192 in 1979 (Hawaii Visitors Bureau 1964, no. 1979). However, the average annual rate of growth of visitors during the 1970s was only half, ten percent, compared to twenty percent for the Golden Age of Jet Travel. Hawaii's stage in the product life cycle was past the rapid growth stage. The substantial reduction in the growth rate of visitors to Hawaii was an indication that Hawaii was reaching the mature stage of the product life cycle.

Mature Stage 1980–1989

In 1980, Hawaii experienced the first decline in total visitors in over thirty years since 1949 (Hawaii Visitors Bureau 1964, no. 1980). The decline was primarily due to a three percent decline in Westbound visitors. Although the number of total visitors remained the same for 1981, westbound visitors declined for the second consecutive year. The decline in westbound visitors was partially due to the double-dip U.S. recessions of 1980 and 1981 (Roos 2020). If eastbound visitors had not continued to increase, there would have been a second year of decline in total visitors (Hawaii Visitors Bureau 1964, no. 1981). This was the beginning of instability in visitor arrivals that Hawaii had never experienced before. Inconsistent growth is one of the signs of the mature stage of the product life cycle for a destination.

Hawaii was fortunate that through deregulation airlines continued to increase their routes to the islands. After leaving in 1978, American Airlines reentered Hawaii routes in 1980. Low–cost carriers entered the Hawaii routes, but fare competition from the major airlines soon drove them out of the market. The low-cost carriers, moreover, were not as reliable as the major airlines.

Consumers soon realized that low fares often meant less service and cancelled or delayed flights.

An unfortunate victim of deregulation was Pan American Airways, which under CAB regulation was allowed primarily international routes. When deregulation occurred, the major domestic carriers such as American and United Airlines had extensive domestic route systems that could feed into international routes. Pan American had only limited domestic routes and was not able to compete effectively with the other major U.S. Airlines. Pan American sold its Pacific routes to United Airlines in 1985 and closed all operations in Honolulu except for its daily around the world flight (Hawaii Aviation 2015a). The pioneer across the Pacific lost its routes in the region which foretold of its eventual demise. An interesting side note is that the seventeen–story Pan Am Building still stands on Kapiolani Avenue in Honolulu as a reminder of the airline's heroic efforts in establishing routes throughout the Pacific and flights around the world.

The Neighbor Islands gained increased access from the mainland through deregulation of entry into routes. United Airlines in 1983 started direct flights from the West Coast to Maui and Kona, and in 1984 to Kauai. Western Airlines followed with direct flights to Maui, which had become the most popular Neighbor Island (Hawaii Aviation 2015a). An adaptation of a well-known phrase often repeated was "Here Today, Gone to Maui" Using jumbo jets on direct flights to the Neighbor Islands did not prove profitable, and United changed its strategy in 1988 to use Honolulu as a mini hub to the Neighbor Islands. There would be one nonstop flight from Los Angeles to Maui and one nonstop flight from San Francisco to Maui. All other flights would connect to the Neighbor Islands through Honolulu as it used to be.

Plans to develop a major resort property, undertake extensive additions, or renovations typically require years of work in advance of completing a project. The plans tend to look at past experience and operating performance as a basis to forecast future trends. Much of the new construction or expansion of hotel properties during the 1980s was based upon the thirty-year trend of ever-increasing tourists to the islands. The initial unexpected small decline in visitors did not deter expansion plans. The Hilton Hawaiian Village opened the Tapa Tower, which was targeted to meetings and conferences with rooms conveniently located above the meeting rooms so that attendees could take the elevators directly from their rooms to their respective meetings or conference (Hilton Hawaiian Village 2020). Halekulani Corporation was planning a new high rise to replace the original hotel and build a second hotel, the Waikiki Parc, across the street. Kyo Ya had plans for a $22 million renovation of the Sheraton Waikiki Hotel, followed by major renovations at all Kyo Ya – owned hotels. The Outrigger Group launched a $125 million renovation program for its chain of hotels. Other hotel owners also decided to renovate their properties in Waikiki to maintain their competitiveness.

Compared to the additions and renovations on Oahu, new resorts were being developed on the Neighbor Islands which would change the landscape of resorts in Hawaii. The first was the Hyatt Regency Maui Resort & Spa, which opened in 1980 (Fischer 2019). The agreement between Chris Hemmeter and Hyatt Hotels to manage the Hyatt Waikiki gave Hemmeter the exclusive rights to develop other projects for Hyatt Hotels in Hawaii. The strategy was to use the Hyatt Regency Waikiki as a hub from which guests could then be sent to stay at other Hyatt Hotels in Hawaii. The rationale for Hyatt management of Kuilima Resort was that they would be able to cross-sell guests from Waikiki to Kuilima (Hawaii Business 1977).

The Hyatt Regency Maui was located oceanfront on Kaanapali Beach. It was designed as a destination resort with extensive gardens, water playgrounds, wildlife, and an art collection (Isotov 2011). The concept was that guests would not have to leave the resort once they arrived, similar to the all-inclusive resort concept of the French Club Mediterranee, but at a stylish level of luxury. The Hyatt Regency Maui had meeting rooms and a ballroom to accommodate corporate meetings, conferences, and incentive groups, which were sponsored by companies to reward their highest performing workers with all-paid luxury vacations.

In 1984, Inter-Island Resorts sold the Maui Surf and Kauai Surf Hotels to Hemmeter. The Maui Surf was redeveloped completely at a cost of $165 million and opened in 1987 as the Westin Maui (Fischer 2019). A new tower with 200 rooms was added, and the existing 556 rooms of the Maui Surf were completely refurbished. Like the Hyatt Regency Maui, the Westin Maui was designed as a destination resort with luxury rooms, restaurants, commercial space, meeting rooms, convention facilities and a spa. A 25,000 square foot swimming pool encompassing pools at different elevations, connected by water slides and waterfalls, was a major attraction of the hotel. Hemmeter redeveloped the Kauai Surf as a destination fantasy resort with ornate decor such as Greek marble columns and statues, European art, extensive man-made lagoons with boat transportation, horse & carriage rides, and a zoo with 200 animals. When the hotel reopened as the Westin Kauai Resort, there was no other hotel like it in Hawaii (Jones 2007).

Hemmeter's grandest project was still yet to come with the $360 million Hyatt Waikoloa Hotel, which opened in 1988 encompassing sixty-two acres of lava covered land, surrounding Waiulua Bay on the Big Island. The plan was to build a tropical oasis within which guests could enjoy carriage rides drawn by Clydesdale horses, a system of boat rides and trams, dolphins, swimming pools, spa treatments, a museum quality art collection, and artifacts from cultures around the Pacific which would become one of the world's largest hotel art collections (Hilton Waikoloa Village 2020). These four mega-resorts were the first of their kind in Hawaii, and none would ever be built again in Hawaii at the grand scale of the Hyatt Waikoloa.

In contrast to the new resorts being developed, the initial decline in visitors brought financial distress to some hotels. In 1981, hotels closed entire wings to reduce operating costs. Hurricane Iwa in 1982 damaged over one thousand rooms on Kauai. There was a one-month strike against United Airlines in 1985, which caused a reduction in the growth of visitors. The U.S. stock market crash of 1987 resulted in a decline in westbound visitors for the year and no growth for the following year (Roos 2020). During the 1980s, domestic visitors from the U.S. mainland declined in three of the years and experienced no growth for one of the years; international visitors declined in two of the years (Hawaii Visitors Bureau 1964, nos. 1980–1989).

With the increased inventory from new resorts opening, these were difficult times for older properties. Amfac decided to exit the hotel industry and sold the Royal Lahaina Hotel, Coco Palms as well as the Kaanapali Beach Hotel. Inter-Island Resorts left the hotel industry by selling its remaining properties, the Kona Surf and Naniloa Hotels. The Kapalua Hotel was sold after six years of consecutive losses totaling $51.6 million (Kephart 1985, 21, 28). Additional turnover in hotel ownership occurred due to a tide of Japanese investments resulting from the devaluation of the U.S. dollar.

What became known as the Plaza Accord was signed in 1985 by the top five of the world's leading economies. These leading economies were commonly referred to as the G-5 nations and included West Germany, France, the United States, Japan, and the United Kingdom (Twomey 2019, 1). The purpose of the Plaza Accord was to force the United States to devalue U.S. currency, because the U.S. large trade imbalances were hurting the other G-5 countries' economies and impeding growth in developing countries. The United States devalued the U.S. dollar approximately fifty percent. As a result of the decline in the value of the U.S. dollar, the Japanese yen in September 1985 went from an exchange rate of 242 yen per dollar to 153 yen per dollar in 1986. Two years later, the exchange rate declined to 120 yen per dollar (Twomey 2019, 2). The change in exchange rates resulted in a doubling of the value of the yen to the dollar, which meant that U.S. assets could be purchased at fifty percent less than what it would have cost before the devaluation of the U.S. dollar. Japanese companies went on a spending spree not only in Hawaii, but also throughout the United States.

In 1986, Azabu Inc. bought the Hyatt Waikiki for $245 million, and paid $232 million for the Kona Lagoon, Ala Moana, and Maui Marriott Hotels. Kumagai Gumi partnered with Herbert Horita to develop the $2 billion Ko Olina Resort in the West Beach Area on Oahu. Dai-ichi paid $51.5 million for the Mauna Lani Bay Hotel. Nittaku paid $6 million for Spencecliff Corporation's restaurant chain. In 1989, the Outrigger group sold six of its twenty-two hotels to Japanese investors. From a seller's viewpoint, hotel owners in Hawaii were receiving premium prices substantially above original costs and generating a high return on their investment. Japanese investors felt that they were paying bargain basement prices discounted at fifty percent.

The devaluation of the U.S. dollar also caused a spike in Japanese travel to Hawaii. In 1985, there were 855,000 Japanese visitors to Hawaii. The number of Japanese visitors increased by ten percent to 944,000 in 1986 and by twenty three percent to 1,161,000 in 1987. Arrivals from Japan then increased at a slower pace for the next two years, reaching 1,319,000 in 1989 (Hawaii Visitors Bureau 1964, nos. 1985–1989). Japan increased its dominance as the largest international market to Hawaii comprising twenty percent of total visitors to the islands.

The Airline Deregulation Act of 1978 had lasting effects throughout subsequent decades. Hawaii initially benefited with group fares bringing millions of tourists to the islands. The entry of thirteen new airlines to Hawaii routes brought fierce competition and lower airfares. Discounted individual fares resulting from deregulation made cheap fares available to everyone. The westbound domestic market began shifting away from group travel to individual travelers. It no longer was necessary to travel as part of a group to enjoy an affordable vacation in Hawaii. The cheap fares provided freedom from rigid group itineraries, and the flexibility to do whatever one enjoyed on vacation. As opposed to the high-income FITs of the Golden Age, the new FITs came from a broad range of income levels seeking budget vacations. Although of benefit to the traveling public, fare competition resulted in the decline of group travel as individual fares were as low as group fares.

The decline in group travel, in turn, negatively impacted tour wholesalers in Hawaii. The number of tour wholesalers had increased with the growth in group travel, but they now were competing for a shrinking group market. Tour companies were staving off bankruptcy, and the tour industry in Hawaii went through a period of consolidation. In 1982, Dave Elmore's company, First Family of Travel, purchased MacKenzie Tours, Hawaii Leisure, Hawaiian Holidays and Aloha Hawaii Travel. The company purchased Inter-Island Tours in 1984, which made it the owner of most of the largest tour companies in Hawaii (Fooks 1997, 8).

In addition, the changes in the group market brought about shifts in the tour industry. Tour wholesalers in Hawaii specialized in selling tours inbound to Hawaii. They had offices on the U.S. mainland to sell their tours through retail travel agents and outbound tour wholesalers located on the mainland. The advantage of achieving large volumes by specializing in a single destination was lost when the group market to Hawaii started to decline. Instead of locating operations at a destination and specializing in only selling inbound tours to a single destination, it became advantageous for tour wholesalers to locate in major markets and develop a series of outbound tours to different destinations (Fooks 1997, 7). If the demand for one destination declined, an outbound tour wholesaler could develop packages to other popular destinations.

A case in point, Pleasant Hawaiian Holidays, which was one of the largest outbound tour wholesalers on the West Coast specializing in tours to Hawaii, eventually became Pleasant Holidays, selling tours to Hawaii, Mexico, Florida, and other popular vacation destinations. Hawaii no longer was the only dream destination being promoted by major outbound tour wholesalers. Other changes in the travel sales distribution system also occurred due to deregulation.

Under CAB regulation, Hawaii had the advantage of one of the lowest fares per mile of all domestic routes in the United States. This advantage was lost when CAB regulation of airfares was done away with. Deregulation, in addition, liberalized the distribution of airline tickets. The CAB regulated not only price, but also who could sell airline tickets other than the airlines themselves. Charter operators, tour operators with the airfare included in their tour packages and retail travel agents were allowed to resell airline tickets only under strict conditions to control open discounting of fares. Deregulation allowed the open discounting of airfares to the public. Airline consolidators like Cheap Tickets became successful by buying bulk fares from airlines and reselling them to the public at fares lower than those offered by the airlines. The discounted fares had restrictive conditions such as no changes in the itinerary or no refunds but still became popular as people were willing to trade-off the restrictions for the lower fares. It became cheap to fly not only to Hawaii, but also to other vacation destinations.

In addition to the instability in arrivals, other signs of Hawaii's mature stage as a destination were evident in the changes in the composition of visitors. For the westbound market, the number of repeat visitors to Hawaii had increased to more than half of all visitors (Hawaii Visitors Bureau 1964, nos. 1980–1989). This was a significant change because repeat visitors tend to stay shorter, spend less and do not do the typical tourist activities which they did on their first trip to Hawaii. As repeat visitors increase, interest in taking tours and visiting tourist attractions tend to decline. The average length of stay in Hawaii declined to less than ten days, and the number of visitors staying in condominiums was increasing. The HVB was looking for new markets in Europe and Asia to sustain growth and attract higher spending visitors, such as corporate meetings, conventions, and incentives. With westbound visitors accounting for seventy percent of all visitors, Hawaii had reached the mature stage of the product life cycle. The average annual growth in visitors had declined to only five percent, reflecting two decades of decline in the growth rate of visitors.

Before leaving this section, it should be noted that during the 1980s Asian economies were growing rapidly, as exemplified by the Asian "Tiger Economies" of Hong Kong, Singapore, Taiwan and South Korea (Chen 2020). Travel within Asia was increasing which motivated the development of hotels and resorts throughout the region. Asian airlines were expanding their routes within the region as well as routes to long-distance destinations outside of the region. The opening of China in 1978 resulted in major investments in tourism facilities by both the Chinese government and foreign investors. Major hotel corporations were anxious to manage properties in China as part of their world-wide network. Sheraton Corporation in 1985 signed an agreement to operate the Great Wall Sheraton Hotel in Beijing, which was the first hotel in China to bear the name of an international hotel company (Encyclopedia.com 2020). The headquarters of Sheraton Pacific in Hawaii was shifted to Hong Kong and expanded as Sheraton Asia-Pacific Division (Chan 2020). The change in the name to Asia-Pacific reflected the focus on Asia as the fastest growing region in tourist arrivals and expenditures. Over the next five years, Sheraton opened four hotels in China. Other developing countries such as Thailand, Malaysia, Indonesia, and India also were looking to develop more tourist facilities in light of increased demand from Europe as well as from within the region. Asian destinations during the 1980s were becoming prominent for both business and leisure travel.

Stagnation 1990–1999

The 1990s was a decade of turmoil beginning with the United States being in a recession due to the failure of thousands of savings and loans institutions during the late 1980s. Iraq invaded Kuwait in 1990, starting the Gulf War, which resulted in a doubling of oil prices. The recession lasted for eight months. At the same time, Japan's Nikkei stock index declined by twenty-five percent and spiraled downward, losing $2 trillion by the end of 1990. The decline in Japanese stocks brought the end of Japan's bubble economy. The Japanese economy would enter a long period of decline, forcing Japanese investors to sell overseas properties to deal with the financial crisis at home.

An effect of the Gulf War was that the U.S. government called on the nation's airlines to support the war efforts in the Middle East by providing aircraft and crew for one of the largest airlifts of troops and equipment. To shift capacity for the war effort, U.S. airlines reduced their capacity flying to Hawaii in 1991 and 1992 (Imbriani 2012). The combination of substantial reductions in airline flights and a major recession in the United States had a negative impact on Hawaii's tourism. In addition, Hurricane Iniki devastated Kauai in 1992 and the first bombing of the World Trade Center occurred in 1993, killing six people and injuring another one thousand persons (Diplomatic Security Article 2019).

During the 1990s, major shifts in transpacific routes were beginning to occur. Although the U.S. airline industry was deregulated, international routes were still regulated by bilateral air agreements between countries. The bilateral air agreements were very restrictive in limiting which carriers could fly specific routes, seat capacity, flight frequency, types of stopovers, picking up passengers, and if passengers could land at a destination. Deregulation of U.S. domestic routes led to liberalization of international routes through the U.S. International Airline Competition Act of 1979 (Cannon 1980).

The introduction in 1988 of the Boeing-747-400 airplanes was a game changer. Airlines during the early 1980s were providing nonstop service across the Pacific rim. The Boeing-747-400 was designed for longer routes, such as flying across the Pacific, with an extended range of 8,357 miles and passenger capacity of 416

(Modern Airliners 2018). Travelers would be able to fly long-distance Pacific routes at affordable fares due to the large passenger capacity of the Boeing-747-400. Instead of stopping over in Hawaii for trips between the Asia-Pacific region and the United States, airlines were bypassing Hawaii to fly more profitable international routes. Singapore Airlines and Malaysian Airlines began to over-fly Hawaii in 1992. United Airlines expanded services in 1993 between the West Coast and the Asia-Pacific region introducing ten new routes, which over-flew Hawaii to provide nonstop service to major gateways in the Asia-Pacific region.

Even though economic regulation of the airline industry was phased out, safety regulations administered by the Federal Aviation Administration (FAA) still prevailed. For safety reasons, aircraft types were limited to fly a maximum range according to the time that it could fly with a disabled engine to an adequate airport for a safe landing. The FAA only allowed jets with three or four engines to fly long-distance, over water routes such as to Hawaii. Advances in aircraft technology producing more powerful jet engines resulted in twin-engine jets that could fly longer distances safely. ETOPS originally referred to **E**xtended-range **T**win-engine **O**perating **P**erformance **S**tandards. It was first introduced in 1985, and the first ETOPS flight was from Boston to Paris under a 120-minute ETOPS rule (Hoke 2015). That is, twin-engine aircraft were allowed to fly no more than 120 minutes flying time away from the nearest airport suitable for an emergency landing. The 120-minute rule was not sufficient for twin-engine aircraft to fly from the U.S. mainland to Hawaii.

The second major change to ETOPS was in 1989, when the FAA extended the ETOPS rule to 180 minutes, making it possible to fly to Hawaii from the U.S. mainland using a twin-engine Boeing 767 jet. This was a positive change for the Neighbor Islands in that airlines now could use twin-engine airplanes to fly nonstop from the West Coast to each Neighbor Island without stopping over in Honolulu. United Airlines began to market each Neighbor Island as a distinct destination. On the other hand, using twin-engine aircraft made it possible for airlines to shift their jumbo jets to lucrative international routes, which generated higher revenues per passenger mile.

The combination of the above events and changes created challenging times for Hawaii's tourism. Total number of visitors declined for three consecutive years from 1990-1993 (Hawaii Visitors Bureau 1964, 1990–93). Business meetings and conventions declined for the sixth consecutive year. Hawaiian Airlines was under new ownership and incurred losses of $120 million. First Family of Travel declared bankruptcy.

Hotel values in Hawaii plummeted as seen in the sale of the Hyatt Regency Waikoloa Resort, built for $360 million and sold for $55 million to Pan Global Partners with Hilton Hotels as a minority partner (Advertiser Staff 2002). Other hotels sold at substantial discounts were the Kahala Hilton, valued at $350 million during the boom of 1986–1989 sold for $50 million; the Westin Kauai, valued at $281 million, sold for $51 million, and the Kauai Resort, valued at $27 million, sold for $4.5 million (Advertiser Staff 1996). Kapalua Bay Hotel filed for bankruptcy and eventually was sold by its Japanese owners for only $19 million, less than one-fifth of its original price. Embassy Suites on Maui, which was Hawaii's first all-suite hotel, filed for bankruptcy.

In contrast to the sale of hotels at distressed prices, luxury hotels that were planned earlier were now opening on all major islands. The Hawaii Prince Hotel was Waikiki's first new property in ten years. The Ihilani Resort & Spa, developed and managed by Japan Airlines, was the first hotel to open at Ko Olina Resort on Oahu. Hilton Hotels began the construction of the $95 million Kalia Tower at the Hilton Hawaiian Village. Castle & Cook's plan to develop the entire island of Lanai as an exclusive resort was beginning to materialize with the opening of the 102– room Lodge at Koele and 248–room Manele Bay Hotel, both to be managed by RockResorts (Walling 2020; Reinhold 1990). Maui would see three new luxury hotels open: The Four Seasons Maui at Wailea, Kea Lani Hotel and Ritz Carlton Kapalua Hotel. The Hyatt Regency Kauai opened at Poipu and the Four Seasons Hualalai opened on the island of Hawaii.

New airline services from Canada, Korea and Japan brought hopes of expanding the visitor market. Canada 3000, a discount charter airline, started service from Vancouver to Kona (Hawaii Aviation 2015b). Deregulation of Japan's airline industry allowed All Nippon Airways (ANA) to fly to Honolulu (Aviation Strategy 1999). Japan Airlines started direct service from Japan to Kona. Asiana Airlines started flying from Korea to Honolulu. The increase in new flights were partially offset by declines in flights by other airlines. Visitor arrivals did not recover fully even with the new airline flights.

Worldwide turmoil continued through the second half of the decade with the Oklahoma bombing, gas attack on Japan's subway and Kobe earthquake in 1995. Israel's prime Minister, Yitzhak Rabin was assassinated. TWA flight 800 exploded over John F. Kennedy Airport, killing 230 people on board. The 1996 Olympic Games was bombed in Centennial Olympic Park, Atlanta, Georgia. U.S. embassies in Kenya and Tanzania were bombed. A major financial event that would affect the pattern of travel to East Asian countries was the Asian Financial Crisis which began in 1997.

The Asian Financial Crisis, in part, was caused by the reversal of the Plaza Accord in 1995 (Staff 2020). The governments of the U.S., Germany, and Japan agreed to allow the U.S. dollar to appreciate relative to the yen and the Deutsche Mark. This, in turn, resulted in the appreciation of East Asian currencies that were pegged to the U.S. dollar. As Japanese and German exports became more competitive due to the increase in the value of East Asian currencies, exports and corporate profits of East Asian countries declined. East Asian governments began to abandon the peg of their currencies to the U.S. dollar and devalued their currencies to promote their exports. Thailand in 1997 was the first country to devalue its currency, the Thai baht. Soon after, other Asian countries followed, and the value of East Asian currencies was devalued by as much as thirty eight percent. East Asian stocks declined as much as sixty to seventy percent. Asian countries affected included Thailand, Malaysia, Indonesia, Singapore, Philippines, and South Korea. Japan was still in an economic downturn due to the burst of its bubble economy (Johnston 2009). The stock market declines were felt in the

United States, Europe, and Russia as the East Asian economies entered a period of negative and/or slow growth.

The appreciation of the U.S. dollar made travel to the United States more expensive, and the depreciation of the East Asian currencies made travel to their respective destinations substantially less expensive. The change in exchange rates was one of the reasons that Japanese preferences shifted to short-haul destinations (Haywood 2013). Asia already was popular with Japanese tourists because it had developed luxury resorts and provided a level of luxury that was unsurpassed in other parts of the world. The devalued currencies made it possible to travel to East Asian destinations at bargain prices to enjoy the beaches, exotic atmosphere, five-star luxury hotels, fine dining, and duty-free shopping available at numerous cities and resorts throughout the respective countries.

Korea and China already were popular destinations for Japanese travelers due to their proximity and attractions. Southeast Asian destinations would soon increase in their popularity to Japanese travelers due to bargain prices for exotic, luxury vacations. Since 1980, Japanese visitors to Hawaii continued to increase each year except for the Gulf War, reaching a peak of 2,216,890 in 1997. After the Asian Financial Crisis, the number of Japanese visitors to Hawaii went into a downward spiral and never was able to regain the peak of over two million visitors.

The 1990s was a period of stagnation where there was essentially no growth in total visitors to Hawaii. There were 6,723,531 total visitors to Hawaii in 1990 and 6,741,037 in 1999 (DBEDT 1999). The average annual growth rate for the decade was 0.5 percent or essentially no growth. There were four years of decline in visitors and the remaining years experienced only marginal growth. Turnover in ownership of hotels continued throughout the decade. Bankruptcies were occurring not only in the hotel sector, but also tourist attractions such as Paradise Park, Sea Life Park and Waimea Valley Park. Given the turmoil and disarray of the decade, Hawaii might be considered fortunate to regain the number of visitors and at least return to 1990 levels by the end of the decade.

Summary

During the 1980s and 1990s, Hawaii's tourism faced challenges that it never experienced before. Visitor arrivals up to 1980 had increased consistently for over thirty years. Thereafter, there was instability and successive years of declines in total visitors to Hawaii. If it were not for the continuous increases in Japanese visitors, Hawaii probably would have entered the decline stage of the product life cycle at the end of the 1990s as opposed to only stagnation. External changes and conditions which were previously favorable in fostering the growth of Hawaii's tourism shifted unfavorably, producing negative impacts upon visitor arrivals and the financial stability of tourist–related businesses in Hawaii.

CAB regulation provided initial advantages to Hawaii's tourism development. Regular fares to Hawaii were among the lowest fare per seat mile compared to other domestic routes. The Transpacific Route Case controlled the number of new airlines approved to serve the islands and assisted in opening Hilo as a second gateway to the islands by requiring airlines to provide direct service from the U.S. mainland to Hilo. CAB approval of inclusive tours provided affordable vacation packages to Hawaii, which opened the market to a larger segment of middle-income Americans as well as inducing travel to the neighbor islands. On the other hand, deregulation allowed any airline to enter Hawaii routes, resulting in intense competition. Airlines were able to stop flying to Hilo and instead fly to Kona where the resorts were located.

Fare competition was allowed and soon resulted in individual fares being as low as group fares. Within a relatively short period, the popularity of group travel declined, and GIT travelers were replaced with a new FIT budget traveler. The decline in group travelers resulted in a change in marketing Hawaii tours by inbound tour wholesalers located in Hawaii to outbound tour wholesalers located at major tourist markets, selling whatever destinations would be the most popular at the time. Hawaii now was only one of the destinations promoted in competition with other popular destinations being packaged by outbound tour wholesalers.

Deregulation in addition brought about the emergence of airline consolidators like Cheap Tickets and online travel agencies (OTA) such as Expedia, which would revolutionize the marketing and selling process of all segments of the travel industry (May 2014, 25). Suppliers such as airlines, hotels and tour companies would have the ability to sell directly to potential travelers through the Internet. The Internet, however, shifted market power from sellers to consumers in terms of knowledge and prices, which increased competition among suppliers. Travelers could find online all the information they needed about destinations and make bookings directly online through consolidators or discount OTAs as well as directly to suppliers offering the best deals. Travelers could compare a vacation in Hawaii with all destinations within a 2,500-mile distance from his/her home and select the destination with the price-quality combination that they preferred.

Improvements in aircraft technology first benefited Hawaii by opening markets located farther away and reducing fares to Hawaii through more efficient and larger aircraft. Further advances in terms of increased range of aircraft made it possible to over-fly Hawaii across the Pacific. Deregulation was followed by liberalization of international routes between the United States and other countries. Airlines could fly nonstop from one side of the Pacific to gateways in Asia or Oceania. Hawaii was not a necessary stopover to refuel, and the larger markets in the major cities of the Pacific Rim were more profitable to serve. Hawaii no longer had the geographical advantage of being the "Crossroads of the Pacific".

The Plaza Accord was favorable to Hawaii's tourism by producing a spike in Japanese travelers; the Asian Financial Crisis would have an unfavorable impact for many years. The second wave of Japanese investors resulting from the devaluation of the U.S. dollar were primarily speculators who within a few years found themselves selling the properties that they bought at premium prices for less than half of what they paid. The burst of Japan's bubble economy was followed by the Asian Financial Crisis, which made travel to Hawaii more expensive due to the appreciation of the U.S. dollar and travel to East Asian countries less expensive due to the devaluation in their currencies. Competition from Asian destinations already was increasing. The devaluation of East Asian currencies made it even more attractive to travel to the luxury resorts and hotels located within Asia as compared to long-distance destinations like Hawaii. The Asian Financial Crisis marked the beginning of a continuous decline in Japanese visitors to Hawaii as tour wholesalers in Japan packaged less expensive tours to other destinations in Asia.

Hawaii was seeking high quality visitors i.e., high spending visitors, but a study showed that during the United Airlines strike, Hawaii lost more affluent visitors than budget visitors. The reason for this is that affluent visitors had the income to change their plans quickly in response to unfavorable conditions compared to budget visitors. With declines in westbound visitors due to recessions on the U.S. mainland, Hawaii was looking to Asia to sustain growth. Increases in Japanese travelers previously offset declines in westbound visitors, however this changed after the Asian Financial Crisis.

Hawaii also was looking to Europe to increase visitor arrivals. A demonstration flight by Lufthansa Airlines flying nonstop 7,436 miles from Frankfurt to Honolulu showed that a direct connection was possible. Nothing further materialized from the demonstration flight as Europeans have a history of travelling to exotic destinations in Africa, Asia, and other parts of the world on low-cost charter tour packages. The $350 million Hawaii Convention Center opened in 1998 to attract meetings, conventions, and exhibitions, but this might have been too little too late as Hawaii had begun experiencing declines in the convention market.

Following maturation and stagnation, the logical sequence in the product life cycle would be decline and revitalization. The next chapter will discuss the decline stage for Hawaii, which was followed by a recovery stage. The term *recovery* is used instead of revitalization. Revitalization implies that Hawaii made substantial improvements to facilities and services to increase its attractiveness as a destination, but this was not the case. Chapter 6 ends with a discussion on long-run trends in Hawaii's tourism which have implications for the future.

Chapter 6

Decline Stage, Recovery, & Long-Run Trends

Overview

By the 1990s, Hawaii's tourism had moved through the introduction, growth and maturation stages of the product life cycle and entered a period of stagnation. Visitor arrivals to Hawaii increased consistently from 1950 to 1990 except for a nominal decrease of less than one percent in 1980. This changed dramatically during the 1990s, when tourist arrivals decreased for four out of the ten years, resulting in a period of no growth. The declines in visitor arrivals were brought about by negative impacts upon Hawaii's tourism from world conditions such as the Gulf War and Asian Financial Crisis. Unstable world conditions continued through the next ten years resulting in wide fluctuations in visitor arrivals as will be discussed in the decline stage of Hawaii's tourism. The recovery stage was brought about by changes in external factors affecting key major markets to Hawaii.

Decline Stage 2000–2009

The decline stage began on a positive note with an increase in visitors to almost seven million in 2000 (DBEDT 1999, no. 2000). United Airlines initiated wide-body Boeing-777 airplane flights to Maui. American Trans Air introduced flights from Los Angeles to Maui, and American Airlines added a flight from San Jose to

Maui. United Airlines also increased its service to Kauai to daily flights. Harlequin Air Corporation initiated charter flights from Japan to Honolulu (Hawaii Aviation 2015). Outrigger Enterprises announced a $300 million redevelopment plan for Waikiki (Hotel Online 2001).

In the following year, the terrorist attacks on the World Trade Center and Pentagon on September 11, 2001, combined with the Dot Com technology bubble burst resulted in almost a ten percent decline in visitors to 6.3 million in 2001. Air travel declined due to the terrorist attacks using hijacked airplanes, and United Airlines filed for bankruptcy protection in 2002. On the other hand, Continental Airlines increased its nonstop service from Houston to Honolulu; Japan Airlines increased its daily flights from Tokyo; and Aloha Airlines began service from Burbank and Vancouver to Honolulu. In 2004, Harmony Airlines initiated daily service from Vancouver to Honolulu and to Maui. Delta Airlines added services from Cincinnati and Atlanta. China Airlines and EVA Air reinitiated flights from Taipei (Hawaii Aviation 2015).

Visitor arrivals remained about the same from 2001-2003 and then experienced three successive years of growth reaching a peak of 7.5 million visitors in 2006. The growth was in part due to a rebound in the U.S. market, which increased from 4.1 million visitors in 2002 to 5.2 million in 2006 (DBEDT 1999, no. 2006). World conditions influenced Americans to travel domestically with the War on Terror declared by President Bush leading to open warfare in Afghanistan and Iraq, and terrorist bombings occurring in Bali, Madrid, Philippines, London, and India. A record heatwave killed over thirty thousand people in Europe in 2002. There was a Severe Acute Respiratory Syndrome (SARS) epidemic in Asia, and an Indian Ocean earthquake killed more than 300,000 people (World Health Organization 2020). Four hurricanes devastated Florida and other parts of the Southern U.S. in 2004, and Hurricane Katrina devastated New Orleans in 2005. The destruction from the hurricanes limited travel to these areas as competing destinations to Hawaii (National Hurricane Center and Central Pacific Hurricane Center 2020).

Canada was the second major market contributing to the 2006 peak in visitors to Hawaii. During the 1970s, the number of Canadian visitors increased to a peak of 311,710 visitors in 1978, declined during the 1980s, and fluctuated with years of declines and growth during the 1990s. Canadian outbound travel tends to coincide with changes in the value of the Canadian dollar (Government of Canada 2017). The exchange rate of the Canadian dollar to the U.S. dollar appreciated by thirty percent from 2000 to 2009. The Canadian dollar was about equal to the U.S. dollar from 2006-2009, which was the highest exchange rate since 1990 (USForex Inc. 2020). Direct flights from Canada to Hawaii increased during the seasonal winter peak travel. Canadian visitors to Hawaii increased thirty-eight percent, from 251,843 visitors in 2000 to 346,583 in 2009 (DBEDT 1999, no. 2009). The insecurity and natural disasters in numerous parts of the world also may have influenced Canadians to select Hawaii over other destinations.

The Global economic downturn in 2007 brought about by the sub-prime mortgage crisis resulted in one of the deepest economic recessions for the United States (Roos 2020). The bankruptcies of major corporations such as Lehman Brothers and General Motors occurred. The U.S. government's $700 billion financial bailout of Fannie Mae and Freddie Mac reflected the severity of the financial crisis and subsequent recession. The United Kingdom's $400 billion banking rescue plan was part of the global economic downturn. Impacted by the deteriorated conditions of the economy, U.S. visitors to Hawaii declined by almost one million visitors over the next three years, from 5,173,264 in 2006 to 4,280,286 in 2009.

Throughout the decade, the Japanese market continued to decline, from 1,817,643 in 2000 to 1,168,080 in 2009. Visitors from developing markets Europe, Other Asia (all Asian countries other than Japan), and Latin America, also declined during the decade. Overall, total visitors to Hawaii declined from 6,948,595 in 2000 to 6,420,448 in 2009. If it were not for the growth in Canadian visitors, the decline stage would have been more severe. The decrease of 649,583 Japanese visitors was a key factor contributing to the decline stage from 2000-2009.

Industry changes that occurred during the decline stage would have far reaching impacts. Major hotel corporations shifted from developing new hotel properties to expanding their timeshare properties as part of their vacation clubs. Developing timeshares was not only profitable, but also reduced the risk and investment for developers (Powanga and Powanga 2008). Marriott converted the Maui Ocean Club to a timeshare in 2000 and opened the Ko Olina Beach Club timeshare in 2003 (Advantage Vacation 2020). Starwood's Vacation Club opened the Westin Kaanapali Resort Villas in 2003 and the Westin Princeville Ocean Resort Villas in 2008 (Vacation Ownership.com 2020). Hilton Grand Vacations opened the Lagoon Tower at the Hilton Hawaiian Village in 2001; converted the Kalia Tower to timeshares in 2003; converted rooms at Waikoloa to timeshares in 2006; opened the King's Land Resort at Waikoloa in 2008; and built the Hilton Grand Waikikian, which opened in 2008 (Hilton Grand Vacations 2020). In addition, condotels were being built instead of regular hotel properties to reduce the risk and investment of developers similar to timeshares. The Beach Villas at Ko Olina, a luxury condominium, opened in 2008 and Trump International Hotel opened in Waikiki in 2009 (Travel Hawaii 2009).

In terms of new aircraft, Singapore Airlines launched the Airbus 380 into service in 2007 (Slotnick 2020). The Airbus 380 is the largest commercial passenger jet airplane in the world. It has two decks and can accommodate 555 passengers in a three-class seating configuration or 853 passengers in an all-economy configuration. The Airbus 380 can fly 8,200 nautical miles and fly nonstop for almost eighteen hours (Airbus 2021). Given its large passenger load and extended range, the A-380 typically was used on high traffic international routes. Middle East airlines such as Emirates provided service from major European cities to Asia, Australia, and New Zealand via Dubai. The A-380 also was used by foreign airlines on U.S. routes to the Middle East and Europe using the polar route in addition to overseas routes. During this time, all of the A-380 routes were to destinations other than Hawaii (Airbus 2020). As a leisure destination, Hawaii routes were not as lucrative as high traffic, long- range international routes.

The post Dotcom bust was followed by technology innovations in search engines and social media which changed how information was gathered and distributed through social media, reaching millions of users on the Internet. Google and Facebook were launched in 2004. YouTube was launched in 2005, and Twitter was launched in 2006. Access to the Internet was made convenient through Apple's debut of the iPhone in 2007. These technological innovations put the search for travel information at a person's fingertips, and personal recommendations from fellow travelers conveniently available through social media. Consumers already had grown wary of advertisements and relied on social media for recommendations, which from reliable sources had more influence on purchase decisions than advertising. Negative comments from social media would reduce the effectiveness of promoting a destination through advertising. Additional innovations discussed in the next section would change the booking process for alternative accommodations in lieu of hotels.

Recovery 2010-2019

The recovery stage was the first time in twenty years that Hawaii experienced consecutive years of increases in visitor arrivals for the entire decade. Visitor arrivals increased at an average annual rate of 4.8 percent, from 6,919,894 in 2010 to 10,282,160 in 2019 (DBEDT 1999, no. 2010,2019). The United States entered its longest period of expansion beginning in June 2009 and ending in early 2020 due to the coronavirus pandemic (Li 2019). Unemployment declined to 3.6 percent, which was the lowest since 1969. The total number of U.S. visitors to Hawaii increased by fifty-two percent from 4,534,851 in 2010 to 6,879,214 in 2019. Visitors to Hawaii from the U.S. West, which encompasses twelve Pacific and mountain states, increased by 58 percent. A contributing factor to the growth in U.S. visitors was the turnaround in visitors from the U.S. East, which covers all the other states in the continental United States. Visitors to Hawaii from the U.S. East was a declining market from 1989 to 2009 but increased 41 percent from 1,610,421 in 2010 to 2,265,012 in 2019.

Continued instability throughout other parts of the world discouraged travelers from visiting the affected areas. Americans were being targeted as reflected in the bombing of the J.W. Marriott and Ritz Carlton Hotels in Jakarta in 2009, the attack on the U.S. Consulate in Pakistan in 2011, and the attack on the U.S. Consulate in Benghazi, where U.S. Ambassador Christopher Stevens was killed. Wars were continuing in Afghanistan, Iraq, and Syria. Terrorist attacks and bombings occurred in Moscow, Norway, Somalia, Paris, and London. In contrast to the prosperity in the United States, there was a European sovereign debt crisis affecting Greece, Spain, Portugal, Ireland, and Cyprus. Riots were occurring across England in 2011. The Arab Spring revolutions were happening in Tunisia, Egypt and Libya, and there were protests in Hong Kong (Kenton 2020; Editors 2020; *BBC News* 2019; Taylor 2011). The "Yellow Vest" movement in France began in 2018 due to the high price of gasoline and continued in 2019 due to pension reform. It was the largest period of civil unrest throughout France since 1958 (Cigainero 2018). Disasters in other parts of the world included the Haiti earthquake; the Fukushima Nuclear Plant meltdown in Japan; the disappearance of Malaysian Airlines flight 370 with 227 passengers and 12 flight crew; and the Sulawesi earthquake and tsunami (World Nuclear Association 2020; The Week Staff 2020; Center 2018).

Parts of the United States also experienced devastating events with the drilling platform explosion in the Gulf of Mexico, which resulted in 134 million gallons of oil spilling into the waters and damaging 1,300 miles of shoreline along five states from Texas to Florida. Hurricane Sandy hit New Jersey and New York in 2012, and Hurricane Harvey hit Texas in 2017, causing about $125 billion in damage. Harvey ranked as the second-most costly hurricane on the U.S. mainland since 1900 (US Department of Commerce 2017; World Vision 2018; National Hurricane Center and Central Pacific Hurricane Center 2020). Hurricanes Irma and Maria followed Harvey affecting Florida, Puerto Rico, and much of the Caribbean, causing another $140 billion in damages.

The United States experienced a series of violent events. A mass shooting occurred in Denver in 2012, followed by the Boston Marathon bombing in 2013. The Charleston church shooting occurred in 2015, and the mass shooting in Las Vegas resulted in fifty-eight deaths in 2017. The shooting at a synagogue in Pittsburg resulted in eleven deaths in 2018 (Brown 2012; Editors 2019; Zapotosky 2017; Choi 2020; Saldivia, Van Sant, and Bowman 2018). The instability throughout the world as well as devastating and violent events in the United States may have influenced Americans as well as international travelers to consider Hawaii as a preferred destination to visit.

After declining for twelve years since 1997, to a low of 1,168,060 visitors in 2009, the Japanese market to Hawaii began to increase in 2010. Japanese outbound travel began to surge after the Fukushima Nuclear Plant meltdown. The Japan Travel Bureau (JTB) Foundation stated that one of the reasons for the surge was "the psychological impact of the quake-related disasters, which may have subconsciously boosted the desire to travel" (Moodie Report 2012, 1). The rate of departures was setting new records especially among young travelers, particularly women in their 20s. The quake-related disasters led to a change in the Japanese younger generation's sense of values regarding overseas travel. Outbound seating capacity was increasing with the expansion of international flights at Haneda Airport since 2010, and the value of the Japanese yen versus the U.S. dollar was relatively high from 2008-2012 (Macrotrends.net 2020). Japanese visitors to Hawaii increased by twenty-five percent, from 1,239,080 in 2010 to 1,545,806 in 2019. Although still less than the peak of 2.2 million visitors in 1997, this was a significant increase in the Japanese market, compared to successive years of decline.

The Canadian market continued its rebound, which began in 2002 and continued for seventeen years. The value of the Canadian dollar remained at high levels, about equal to the U.S. dollar from 2010 to 2014 (USForex Inc. 2020). West Jet began using wide-body Boeing-767 airplanes for seasonal nonstop flights in 2016 from Edmonton and Calgary to Maui and Honolulu (WestJet 2016). The nonstop flights encouraged increased travel to Hawaii from cities beyond Vancouver. In 2019, West Jet elevated the quality of its flights by introducing Boeing-787 Dreamliner flights with 320 seats in a three-seat configuration from Calgary to Maui (Calgary International Airport 2019). During the seasonal winter months, West Jet operated the most flights from Canada to Hawaii with twenty-two weekly flights from Western Canada (Vancouver, Edmonton, and Calgary) to Maui, and twenty-eight weekly flights from Vancouver to Honolulu, Lihue, and Kona. With a higher exchange rate for the Canadian dollar and substantially increased access, Canadian visitors increased 32 percent, from 405,040 in 2010 to 535,267 in 2019.

In regard to technological innovations, Apple introduced its iPad in 2010 and smart watch in 2015, which increased the convenience and ease of accessing the Internet on a real-time basis. The booking app, Airbnb, was launched earlier in 2007, but growth in bookings was not experienced until after it changed its name to Airbnb in 2009 and received investor funding for expansion (Airbnb 2016). Airbnb is an online marketplace where people can rent out their homes or spare rooms to visitors. Airbnb charges a commission to owners for every booking in addition to commissions charged to visitors renting the accommodations. The app made it convenient for millions of people throughout the world to rent their homes or spare rooms to earn additional income. Airbnb has operations in 191 countries and has over two million listings worldwide.

For Hawaii, the number of vacation rental units increased from 1,355 in 2000 to 6,719 in 2009 and to 13,555 in 2019 (Hawaii Tourism Authority 2020). Over one million visitors to Hawaii stayed in rental homes and Bed & Breakfasts during 2019. Vacation rentals have been a problem for years and became a major issue in 2019. Most vacation rentals were illegal in terms of not having the required permits and licensing for rentals less than thirty days. The illegal vacation rentals were in residential areas causing traffic, parking, rubbish, and noise problems for residents.

The hotel industry continued expansion into timeshares with the 2011 opening of Aulani, a Disney Resort and Spa, in Ko Olina, Oahu. Hilton Grand Vacations opened the Hokulani Waikiki in 2013 (Paiva 2010; Hilton Grand Vacations 2020). The Sheraton Kauai was converted in 2015 to a timeshare as part of Sheraton's

Vacation Club. The Waikoloa Ocean Club opened in 2017 as part of Marriott's Vacation Club. Marriott offered 307 fee-simple luxury condominiums at its Ritz–Carlton Residences in Waikiki with its Ewa Tower opening in 2016 and an additional 245 units at its Diamond Head Tower in 2018 (Ritz–Carlton 2020). The price of the resort residences ranged from $1 million to $20 million for a penthouse. The studios, suites and penthouses also could be booked by visitors for short–term stays. Overall, the shift toward vacation rentals and timeshares reflects long-run trends in visitors which are discussed in the next section.

Long-run Trends 1990–2019

Long-run analysis provides a comprehensive view for identifying key trends that affect the nature of Hawaii's tourism. The analysis primarily covers twenty-nine years, 1990–2019. Earlier years are included in the analysis to the extent that complete data are available for comparison purposes. The long-run trend in total visitors already has been covered in the previous chapters on the stages of Hawaii's tourism life cycle. Seven key trends are discussed in this section: 1) visitors from major market areas, 2) visitors from developing markets, 3) first-time versus repeat visitors, 4) visitors to Hawaii for a convention, corporate meeting, or incentive travel, 5) visitor accommodations, 6) visitors by island, and 7) visitor expenditures.

Visitors from major market areas

The United States has always been the primary source of visitors to Hawaii. Since 1990, visitors from the United States have fluctuated over the years due to recessions and other negative world conditions but have increased steadily during the recovery stage to almost seven million visitors. In 2019, the United States accounted for 67.1 percent of total visitors to Hawaii. The next largest visitor market to Hawaii was Japan with 15.4 percent of total visitors, followed by Canada with 5.3 percent.

For Japan, the peak number of visitors in 1997 has yet to be recovered. Visitors from Japan declined by one million visitors from 2,216,890 in 1997 to 1,168,080 in 2009. Visitors from Japan increased to 1,545,806 in 2019, however, this was only about equal to the number of visitors from Japan in 1990. For the most part, Japan has been a declining or stagnant visitor market to Hawaii. The growth in the number of Japanese visitors during Hawaii's recovery stage reflected changes in external conditions fostering outbound Japanese travel, which may not continue into the future.

As mentioned previously, Canadian visitors reached an early peak in 1978 with 311,710 visitors. It was not until 2007 that visitors from Canada recovered to 333,397 visitors. Since then, visitors from Canada experienced almost continuous growth to 535,267 visitors in 2019, but Canadian visitors comprise only a small proportion of total visitors to Hawaii. The United States and Japan account for 82.5 percent of all visitors to Hawaii.

As defined by the HTA, there are four major market areas (MMAs) of visitors to Hawaii – the U.S. West, U.S. East, Japan, and Canada. As noted previously, the U.S. West MMA includes twelve Pacific and mountain states, and the U.S. East MMA includes all other states in the continental United States. From 1990–2019, the U.S. West has been the only MMA with consistent growth throughout the years. The U.S. West accounted for half of all U.S. visitors in 1990 and increased to two-thirds of all U.S. visitors in 2019. The number of visitors from the U.S. East has been declining or stagnant. It was not until 2017 that the number of visitors from the U.S. East exceeded that of 1990. Three out of the four major MMAs – the U.S. East, Japan, and Canada – were declining or stagnant visitor markets to Hawaii for most of the years from 1990–2019.

Visitors from developing markets

Visitors from Europe, Oceania and Other Asia were considered developing international markets that have the potential for growth in visitors to Hawaii. Other Asia includes all Asian countries other than Japan. Throughout the years, Hawaii has looked towards Europe to supplement growth in visitors to Hawaii. Europe has been a declining or stagnant market since 1992. Europe accounted for only one percent of total visitors to Hawaii in 2019. After over twenty-five years of no growth, one can conclude that Europe will not be a significant visitor market for Hawaii. Europeans have numerous destinations to select from throughout Europe, the Americas, and Asia versus traveling to Hawaii.

Total visitors from developing international markets in general declined from 1992-2009 until visitors from Oceania and Other Asia began to experience consistent growth. Australia was the country accounting for most of the growth from Oceania. South Korea accounted for most of the growth from Other Asia. Residents from China, the top tourism spender in the Asia-Pacific region, have not developed into a major source of visitors to Hawaii. Total visitors from developing international markets accounted for less than ten percent of all visitors to Hawaii in 2019.

First-time versus repeat visitors

The trends in first-time versus repeat visitors are of interest not only for promotional strategies, but also for the differences in their respective expenditure patterns at a destination. In 1989, repeat visitors equaled first-time visitors and continued to increase more than first-time visitors over the next thirty years. First-time visitors declined by over one million visitors, from 3,299,065 in 1990 to 2,185,039 in 2009. During the ten years of consecutive growth from 2010-2019, first-time visitors reached 1990 arrivals of 3,290,291 showing no growth for almost thirty years. On the other hand, repeat visitors more than doubled, from 3,424,466 visitors in 1990 to 6,991,869 in 2019, accounting for 68 percent of all visitors.

Based on information available for 2019, the average number of trips for repeat visitors was 7.2. The majority of visitors from the four major MMAs were repeat visitors – 80.6 percent for the U.S. West, 68.3 percent for Japan, 64.6 percent for Canada, and 58.5 percent for the U.S. East. Almost all, 81.3 percent, of repeat visitors came for a vacation and 9.6 percent visited friends and relatives. As might be expected, almost all, 78.3 percent, of repeat visitors made their own travel arrangements, because they were already familiar with Hawaii.

Expenditures per person for repeat visitors from the four major MMAs were only a little less than that for first-time visitors – $231 per person for Japanese repeat visitors versus $264 for first-time Japanese visitors, $205 versus $213 for U.S. East, $171 versus

$182 for U.S. West, and $156 versus $176 for Canada (DBEDT 1999, no. 2019). Differences in the composition of expenditures, however, can result in different net benefits to Hawaii, as discussed in the section on visitor expenditures. Given the high number of repeat trips and familiarity with Hawaii, general promotional efforts by the HTA would not be as effective towards attracting repeat visitors compared to improvements in their experience while visiting Hawaii. Improving the experience of visiting Hawaii, moreover, would be beneficial to attracting first-time visitors.

Conventions, corporate meetings & incentive travel

Conventions, corporate meetings, and incentive travel are considered segments of the business travel market, which can be influenced to travel to a destination that meets their respective requirements. Conventions or conferences are meetings of members of a particular group such as the annual meetings of national or international associations. Corporate meetings in this context refer to away from home meetings organized by a company to bring together executives and staff from different locations such as a regional corporate meeting. Incentives are rewards provided by a company to employees for their exceptional performance. An all-expense paid vacation is among the highest rewards that can be earned. Corporate meetings and incentive travel typically are handled by specialists in travel companies as well as by in-house corporate staff in the case of large corporations. In addition, major hotel companies have departments that specialize in providing services for conventions, corporate meetings, and incentive travel.

The convention market has never been a significant market segment for Hawaii. Except for a few years, the number of convention visitors has been a declining or stagnant market since 1990. The number of convention visitors in 2019 was 230,716, which was less than the 265,180 in 1990. Convention visitors accounted for only 2 percent of total visitors to Hawaii in 2019. The opening of the Hawaii Convention Center in 1998 did not have a sufficient impact to reverse the long-run declining trend in convention visitors. Visitors coming to Hawaii for corporate meetings or incentive travel also did not substantially increase over the years, and, similar to convention visitors, are marginal components of total visitors to Hawaii. Efforts to expand the business travel market to Hawaii have not been successful.

Visitor accommodations

Over the last twenty years, the composition of visitor accommodations in Hawaii has changed dramatically. The number of hotel properties declined from 161 in 2000 to 148 in 2019 (Hawaii Tourism Authority 2020). The decline in properties reflects the hotel industry's shift toward timeshares by converting existing hotel rooms to timeshares as well as building new timeshare properties. The number of timeshare properties almost doubled, from 45 in 2005 to 87 in 2019. In terms of units or rooms, hotel rooms declined, from 50,681 in 2000 to 43,217 in 2019, whereas timeshare units increased from 6,026 in 2004 to 12,090 in 2019. Another major shift in visitor accommodations was the increase in vacation rental units, from 1,867 in 2004 to 13,555 in 2019. The number of vacation rental units may be underestimated since many vacation rentals are illegal and are not likely to respond to requests for information.

From accounting for 71 percent of all visitor accommodations in 1990, hotels now account for only 54 percent of visitor accommodations. Condotels account for 13 percent of all visitor accommodations; timeshares account for 15 percent; and vacation rentals account for 17 percent. In terms of usage, approximately 60 percent of visitors stayed in a hotel during their visit in 2019, 17 percent stayed in a condominium, 8 percent stayed in a timeshare, and 15 percent stayed in alternative accommodations such as vacation rentals, which include rental homes, B & B's, and rooms in private homes.

The advent of Airbnb and other vacation rental apps opened the market for alternative accommodations, which are less expensive than staying at hotels. The number of visitors staying in timeshares may be underestimated because timeshares also are rented as hotel rooms, and visitors staying at a condotel may not realize that they are staying in a condominium being rented as a hotel room. In terms of expenditures, visitors staying at hotels tend to have the highest expenditures. The shift toward timeshares and vacation rentals in part reflect the trend in repeat visitors staying in timeshares and vacation rentals.

Visitors by island

Although Hawaii is comprised of eight major islands, four of the islands, Oahu, Maui, Kauai, and Hawaii island, receive almost all of the visitors. As mentioned previously, Kahoolawe is uninhabited. Niihau is privately owned, and visitors are allowed only by invitation. Billionaire, Larry Ellison owns 98 percent of the island of Lanai, which has two Four Seasons Resorts. It is of interest to note that Ellison paid only $300 million for almost all of Lanai (Martin 2017). This was less than the $360 million Chris Hemmeter invested to develop the Hyatt Waikoloa Resort in 1988 and less than the $350 million for constructing the Hawaii Convention Center. The number of visitors to Lanai is limited by capacity. Visitors to Lanai increased from 46,052 in 1990 to 87,545 in 2019. Residents of Molokai prefer not to have large scale tourism. Since 1990, the number of visitors to Molokai has declined from 103,477 in 1990 to 65,055 in 2019.

The most popular island is still Oahu, followed by Maui, Hawaii island, and Kauai. Oahu is the favorite destination of first-time and repeat visitors. Almost three-fourths of first-time visitors stay on Oahu, and over half of repeat visitors stay on Oahu. The popularity of Oahu would be expected with Waikiki Beach, shopping centers, major attractions, and events on the island. Oahu also has the largest capacity to host tourists in terms of tourist facilities. Visitors to Oahu increased by 20 percent, from 5,139,558 in 1990 to 6,193,027 in 2019.

The popularity of Maui has continued to increase throughout the years. Visitors to Maui increased by 37 percent, from 2,235,701 in 1990 to 3,071,596 in 2019. With the continuous eruptions of Kilauea Volcano up to 2018, the number of visitors to Hawaii island increased by 58 percent, from 1,127,373 in 1990 to 1,779,526 in 2019. Almost all of the visitors to Hawaii island, 88 percent, stay on the Kona side where the major resorts are located. Hilo has never developed into a major destination area despite early efforts in building a jet runway and the CAB requiring new airlines to fly direct flights to Hilo from the U.S. mainland. The two–way flow of visitors throughout the State never came to pass.

Kauai has been fortunate to recover from two hurricanes, Hurricane Iwa in 1982 and Hurricane Iniki in 1992, which was one of the most damaging hurricanes in the East Central Pacific. Visitors to Kauai have remained about the same over the last twenty-nine years, with 1,228,850 visitors in 1990 and 1,374,944 visitors in 2019.

Visitor expenditures

One of the most important reasons for developing tourism is to generate income and employment from the expenditures of visitors. Visitor expenditures can be presented in current dollars, which would be referred to as *nominal* visitor expenditures, or adjusted for inflation, which would be referred to as *real* visitor expenditures. Adjusting visitor expenditures for inflation would eliminate the effects of price level changes so that the *real* changes in the amount of physical goods that were bought can be compared over time to obtain a true picture of trends in expenditures.

The number of visitors increased from 6,488,422 in 1989 to 10,282,160 in 2019. Real visitor expenditures reached a peak in 1989 (Brewbaker 2020). As visitor arrivals have increased, real visitor expenditures have declined until recent years, but are still below the peak of 1989. This is a critical issue because it means that more visitors have not resulted in increased *real* visitor expenditures. With four million more visitors since 1989, the *real* amount of physical goods and services that visitors buy today are less than that of 1989. Increasing the number of visitors has not generated increases in *real* economic benefits i.e., adjusted for inflation.

In addition to the decline in real visitor expenditures, changes in the composition of expenditures will result in different net benefits of visitor expenditures. The shift to other types of accommodations reflects changes in the types of visitors who have different expenditure patterns. For example, visitors who stay in condominiums and time shares spend less at restaurants and dinner shows than those who stay at hotels. An earlier study showed that the trip expenses per person was lower for visitors staying in timeshares than those staying with friends and relatives who stayed longer and spent more on shopping. Visitors staying in condominiums had the highest trip expenditures per person because of their substantially higher length of stay. Visitors in condominiums had an average length of stay of twenty-three days compared to fifteen days for those staying with friends and relatives, eleven days for those staying in timeshares and eight days for those staying in hotels (Choy 2011).

Visitor expenditures on goods and services produced by different sectors of an economy will have different net economic impacts. The magnitude of the net economic impact will depend upon a sector's linkages to other parts of the economy, and the amount of imports used to produce its products or services. To measure the yield or net economic impact of expenditures of visitors to Hawaii, Pratt developed a computable general equilibrium (CGE) model of Hawaii using DBEDT's 2005 Hawaii input-output table and data on annual visitors to Hawaii (Pratt 2012). The results showed that visitors staying in timeshares generated lower economic benefits because their purchases had a higher import content. The study also concluded that on a per day basis Japanese visitors produced the highest net economic benefits, but on a per person basis U.S. East visitors provided the highest net economic benefits. To increase the yield from visitor expenditures, the results suggested that tourism sectors of the economy needed to strengthen backward linkages to other sectors of the economy.

Summary

The decline and recovery of Hawaii's tourism were due to external world conditions beyond Hawaii's control. The rapid and wide fluctuations in visitor arrivals brought about by terrorist attacks, global economic downturns, and disasters are not responsive to promotional efforts and are difficult, if not impossible, to forecast. The hotel industry shift towards timeshares and condotels reflect financial considerations of developers as well as long-run trends in changes in visitor preferences. Innovations in technology and new applications have facilitated the booking of alternative accommodations, which are less expensive than hotels.

Real-time information on destinations is readily available to plan vacations and select which destinations to visit. The Internet has shifted market power to the consumer by providing comprehensive information and facilitating booking travel arrangements online. Travel suppliers, as well as destinations, have substantially less influence on travelers' choices and purchasing decisions except to offer the best value for their dollar. In addition, competition among destinations has increased due to availability of rates and fares through online travel agencies and booking sites that specialize in discounted rates to travel and stay anywhere in the world.

The traditional major visitor markets to Hawaii have remained the same throughout the years. The United States, Japan and Canada generate almost all of the visitors to Hawaii. Three out of the four MMAs of visitors to Hawaii have been declining or stagnant markets for most of the years from 1990-2019. Efforts to increase visitors from Europe have not been successful. China has not developed into a significant market despite nonstop flights from Shanghai. Visitors from developing markets also have not increased substantially over the years and account for only a marginal share of total visitors to Hawaii.

Throughout the years, Hawaii has not been able to increase the number of convention visitors. Longer travel time and higher costs compared to competitive venues closer to home have made it difficult to develop the convention market to Hawaii. The Hawaii Convention Center has been operating at a loss since its inception. A discussion of the Convention Center is presented in the next chapter as part of tourism planning and promotion. Corporate meetings and incentives also have not grown substantially over the years. The meetings, convention and incentive market segment accounted for less than 5 percent of all visitors in 2019.

The popularity of the Neighbor Islands has increased over the years, especially for Maui and Hawaii island, but Oahu remains the most popular island. Increases in the number of visitors have resulted in strains upon the islands' infrastructure and natural environment, crowding and conflicts between residents' needs versus visitors' activities. With less *real* visitor expenditures from increasing numbers of visitors, the situation has posed a major dilemma for future directions, which are discussed in Chapter 9.

Chapter 7

Tourism Planning & Promotion

Overview

Tourism planning is done at different levels of government, as well as by the private sector (Routledge 1994; Choy 1991). The same is true for tourism promotion. Although both to some extent are interrelated, the two functions will be dealt with separately in this chapter to focus on the complexities involved with each one. Planning traditionally is considered one of the four functions of management i.e., planning, organizing, leading, and controlling (American Intercontinental University 2020). Promotion is one of the traditional four Ps of marketing i.e., product, price, place or distribution, and promotion. Since tourism is a service industry, the three additional Ps for services marketing are people, process, and physical evidence (Professional Academy 2020). As will be seen, Hawaii's tourism planning and promotion was limited in scope compared to the broader context of the four functions of management and seven variables of services marketing.

Tourism Planning

Early tourism planning was supply-oriented in terms of providing the infrastructure and facilities for developing destination areas. Prior to the 1950s, developing tourism was a simple process of building facilities, providing transportation access, and promoting a destination (Wahl 2013; Inskeep 1991). The beginnings of early resorts in the United States saw the private sector taking the lead in linking transportation to unused land so that an area could be developed to build tourist facilities. For Atlantic City, a group of businessmen secured a railroad charter and constructed the Camden-Atlantic Rail Line, connecting Philadelphia to Atlantic City (Atlantic City Free Public Library 2020). The city was incorporated in March 1854, and the first public train left Camden, New Jersey, for Atlantic City in July. Camden was located directly across the Delaware River from Philadelphia. The success of Atlantic City was due to its location near large population centers and inexpensive train travel, which made it one of the most popular vacation resorts from the 1850s to 1940s.

The development of Florida as a vacation destination is the story of Henry Flagler and his Florida East Coast Railway (Flager Museum 2020). Flagler co-founded Standard Oil with partners John D. Rockefeller and Samuel Andrews. In the 1800s, Flagler purchased railroads within Florida, eventually building a comprehensive rail system and constructing hotels along the rail line to attract vacationers from the north to enjoy the Florida sunshine and beaches. Flagler's railroad system reached West Palm Beach by 1894. He constructed the Hotel Royal Poinciana in what is now known as Palm Beach, and The Breakers Hotel on the ocean side of Palm Beach. The hotels and railroad access soon established Palm Beach as a winter resort for the wealthy. The Hotel Royal Poinciana became the world's largest resort at that time (Flager Museum 2020, 2).

Landowners further south of Palm Beach convinced Flagler to extend the railway to Biscayne Bay in exchange for land (Greater Miami Convention & Visitors Bureau 2020). In 1896, the railway reached Biscayne Bay, the largest and most accessible harbor on the East Coast of Florida, and the city of Miami was incorporated in the same year. Several years later, private investors started the development of Miami Beach. Originally, Miami Beach was a sandbar and mangrove swamp. Investors had to drain the mangrove swamp, dig deep channels around the sandbar, and fill the sandbar with soil to create Miami Beach. A bridge connecting Miami Beach to the mainland was completed in 1912, and the city of Miami Beach was incorporated in 1915 (Viglucci 2015). During the 1920s, Miami Beach boomed, and hotels were filled as soon as they were built. As a side note, the City of Miami Beach still must dredge sand to refill the beaches because the beaches were artificially constructed (Munzenrieder, Kyle 2015). A substantial portion of South Florida is drained swampland.

For Hawaii, the connection between railroads building hotels and resorts was evident with the construction of the Haleiwa Hotel by the OR&L in 1899 (Chong 1963, 117–18). This followed the pattern of railroads building hotels along their rail lines, which occurred earlier in Europe and then the United States, as was the case for Atlantic City and Miami. The invention of the automobile and its wide acceptance eliminated the advantage of inexpensive rail travel, which negatively affected both Atlantic City and the Haleiwa Hotel. Atlantic City went through several changes including approving gambling to survive. The Haleiwa Hotel eventually closed.

The first plan most often cited in regard to Waikiki is the *Reclamation of the Waikiki District of the City of Honolulu*, completed in 1906 by L.E. Pinkham, who was the President of the Board of Health (Pinkham 1906). At the time, Waikiki was primarily duckponds and swamps, and there was concern about the unsanitary conditions and mosquitoes. Pinkham's plan was essentially urban planning to increase the area of Honolulu for residential development. In his plan, Pinkham cites the success of Boston filling in the Back Bay beginning in 1856 to construct a new neighborhood on wasteland (Back Bay Association 2020).

Pinkham's plan included the dredging of a "*great lagoon*" to secure the material for filling in the duck ponds and swamps. The lagoon would provide an opportunity to create a " *Venice in the midst of the Pacific*" (Pinkham 1906, 12). Ocean water would enter from the beach past Kapiolani Park and exit at the Ala Moana Bridge. There would be boulevards and streetlights on both sides of the lagoon. Pinkham included in his plan a residence park system to account for streets, sidewalks, utilities, and residential lots on the reclaimed land. Although unhealthy conditions were used as the reason for draining the duck ponds and swamplands, it is evident in the plan that the underlying reason was to reclaim the land for development.

About the same time, the U.S. military was interested in building a military installation in Kalia near Waikiki Beach. The military started to reclaim land in 1909 (Young 2014). It took over one year to dredge ocean sediment and pump it to fill the fishponds in the area. The installation was named Fort DeRussy. The Reclamation Canal would be much larger than what was done at Fort DeRussy, but the Fort DeRussy project showed that reclaiming land in Waikiki was feasible. The success of reclaiming land for Miami Beach in 1915 demonstrated that a large project like the Reclamation Canal could be successfully done. It would be another six years before dredging of the Reclamation Canal would start, and the Canal was not completed until 1928.

As discussed above, Hawaii was able to draw upon the experiences of other areas in planning the expansion of Honolulu. Pinkham's plan drew upon the urban planning of Boston's Back Bay. Tourism planning was essentially urban planning focused upon developing tourist facilities (Wahl 2013, ii). One of the first master planned resort communities in the United States was Sea Pines Plantation on Hilton Head Island, South Carolina (The Cultural Landscape Foundation 2020). Charles Fraser wanted to design a resort that respected the environment, and he formed Sea Pines Company in 1956. Fraser hired Hideo Sasaki, who created the master plan for Sea Pines Plantation, which was sensitive to the island's topography, environment, and residents' needs (Retire Hilton Head .com 2020). Sasaki's master plan served as a model for resort planning worldwide. It was during this same time that plans in Hawaii were being made to develop Wailea, Kaanapali and Kona. The private sector would continue to take the lead in master planning and developing resorts in Hawaii throughout the years.

In 1957, the Governor's Advisory Committee on the Tourist Industry published a report, *The Role of Government in The Development of Hawaii's Visitor Industry* (The Governor's Advisory Committee on the Tourist Industry 1957). The report contained an outline of the areas of government action that the committee recommended were necessary to insure the continued growth of the tourist industry in Hawaii. The report was developed based on assumptions, which recognized that:

- Hawaii must not sacrifice community and cultural values basic to the welfare of Hawaii's people.
- Hawaii must provide more in visitor satisfaction than competing destinations.
- The central role of government in the development of tourism is the efficient performance of those functions that are the sole responsibility of government.
- Government development of tourist facilities must be based on benefits exceeding the expenditures of government for the facilities.
- Promote the general welfare; in particular, maximize income and employment in the industry.
- Government facilities must move forward in balance with the growth in visitors.
- Maximize the overall effectiveness of Hawaii in creating visitor satisfaction (The Governor's Advisory Committee on the Tourist Industry 1957, 1).

The report identified the functions of government in the development of tourism as publicity, development of public facilities, maintenance of standards, and the encouragement of community and cultural activities. The report also recognized the need for new destination areas on the Neighbor Islands: "*If tourism in Hawaii continues to expand at its present rate of growth, we will require the equivalent of two additional 'Waikikis within the next ten to twelve years*" (The Governor's Advisory Committee on the Tourist Industry 1957, 19).

Because of the numerous scenic sites on the Big Island of Hawaii, it was expected that the Big Island would eventually rival

Waikiki as a tourist center. Kona was thought to be the most important tourist area outside of Waikiki, and the report recommended that a Kona Coast Scenic Highway be built from the City of Refuge to Kawaihae to "*make the small crescent beaches in the lava flow sections available to visitors and residents for picnicking and swimming*" (The Governor's Advisory Committee on the Tourist Industry 1957, 24). Maui also was considered an important part of tourism development. The report identified facilities that were needed by each island. Two years later, the State Office of Tourism was directed to undertake a study on visitor destination areas in Hawaii.

The State Planning Office contracted John Child & Company to survey the characteristics of successful and unsuccessful destination areas outside of Hawaii and advise the State on policies and programs to "*achieve the maximum investment of private capital in resort accommodations throughout the State with the maximum potential for the success of Hawaii's visitor industry*" (Hawaii. State Planning Office 1960, pt. 2). The survey was completed in 1960 with a list of recommendations based upon the experience of thirteen successful destinations and three unsuccessful areas. One of the recommendations was a list of twelve specifications of a destination area to be used as criteria to identify potential visitor destination areas in Hawaii (Hawaii State Planning Office 1960). The criteria were:

- best possible climate, sunshine, temperature, gentle winds
- attractive natural setting, view, flora
- planned minimum of 1500 rooms
- good sandy beach, calm waters for water sports
- small boat harbor facilities

- conference, auditorium space for conventions
- variety of sports facilities, especially championship golf course
- historic attractions
- close to existing shopping center or developed
- adequate land for development
- staging of at least one traditional activity annually
- continued promotion...$200,000 to $300,000 required annually for each resort

The study recommended a program of public improvements costing approximately $47 million over a six-year period for developing visitor destination areas especially on the Neighbor Islands (Hawaii State Planning Office 1960, pt. 1). Of the total $47 million, only fourteen percent would be spent on improvements for Oahu. A *First Stage Plans for Public Improvements* was completed by Belt, Collins and Associates, and Harland Bartholomew & Associates to identify the specific public improvements to be made on each island. It is not clear whether the areas identified in the study met all twelve criteria for development as visitor destination areas, however, many of the areas identified in the report have been developed as major visitor destination areas in Hawaii.

Thus far, tourism planning in Hawaii was being done by the private sector creating master plans for resorts with the State government assisting in providing the necessary infrastructure for development of specific areas, especially on the Neighbor Islands. The situation became more complex when the General Plan of the State of Hawaii was approved in 1961, establishing the State Land Use Law (State of Hawaii Land Use Commission 2020). All land in Hawaii was classified into four land use districts– urban, rural, agriculture and conservation. The State Land Use Commission (LUC) classified the land and processed petitions to change the boundaries of the classifications. The State Department of Land & Natural Resources was responsible for zoning and managing uses within the conservation district. Each county was responsible for the zoning and managing uses within the urban, rural and agriculture districts.

Development plans by the private sector would have to meet the requirements of all State and County government laws as well as applicable Federal laws. The increased complexity did not seem to deter further development as plans were made for the Kohala Coast Resort Region, and Alexander & Baldwin purchased the land in Wailea from Matson to pursue its plans for a resort community in the area. Up to this point in time, the main purpose of tourism planning in Hawaii was economic development. State planning was done to support the growth of tourism to generate income and employment.

A major assumption of the 1957 report on The Role of Government was that government development of tourist facilities must be based on benefits exceeding costs, but this aspect was not addressed (The Governor's Advisory Committee on the Tourist Industry 1957, 1). It simply was assumed that generating more income and employment would exceed the costs of government developing facilities to support the growth of tourism. A broader view would be to consider the public revenue and costs directly or indirectly generated by visitor activity. This approach was done in the 1970 study, *The Visitor Industry and Hawaii's Economy: A Cost-Benefit Analysis* (Mathematica 1970).

The analysis of the study suggested:

- Visitors to Hawaii easily pay back their costs to the state government.
- The current benefit-cost ratio in regard to the public sector is well above break-even.
- Net private income provided by visitor expenditures is substantial.
- Visitor demand contributes to inflationary pressure as would any other source of demand.
- Over the long-run, visitors as well as residents will contribute to Hawaii's environmental problems.
- Current high benefit-costs ratios may be expected to fall in the future.
- Benefit-cost ratios would fall with a higher proportion of immigrant labor.
- Although the benefit-cost ratios for high-income visitors are in general high, this group is vulnerable to rising costs.
- Current benefit-cost ratios for high–income visitors are slightly lower than benefit cost ratios for middle–income visitors. This differential is likely to increase in the future.

The cost-benefit study provided evidence that suggested that public revenues exceeded public costs associated with visitor activity, but the study did not directly deal with social or environmental impacts of visitor activity. The study also raised an interesting question as to whether the high-income visitor or middle-income visitor would be of more benefit to Hawaii in the future. The study was followed by a series of studies, reports, and legislative actions throughout the 1970s, culminating in the 1978 State Tourism Study.

The State Tourism Study was done in response to the Interim Tourism Policy passed in 1976 (Hawaii. Office of Tourism 1978). The legislation mandated the DPED to develop a ten-year plan for tourism to meet the following State policy objectives:

- Provide the greatest possible satisfaction and quality of service to visitors.
- Protect Hawaii's natural beauty.
- Promote a better understanding by visitors and residents of Hawaii's heritage as well as the cultural and social contributions to Hawaii of all its ethnic groups and peoples.
- Sustain the economic health of the visitor industry to the extent that such economic growth is compatible with the aforesaid objectives.

The Study consisted of five documents: physical resources, public revenue-cost analysis, economic projections, manpower and an executive summary. The economic projections provided some controversy because the projections were misunderstood and taken out of context. The projections were generated by a simulation model to assess what outcomes would result from different rates of growth in visitors. Using 1975 as the base year, four assumed rates of growth were used: zero growth, 5 percent, 10 percent, and 15 percent. The highest growth rate of 15 percent projected 5.7 million visitors for 1980 and 11.5 million for 1985. These numbers were taken out of context and treated as what would actually happen versus projections being used for evaluating different scenarios.

The number of visitors resulting from the assumed rates of growth was used to project the number of additional hotel rooms that would be needed to meet visitor demand by island and in turn, the number of additional jobs created. The analysis using the simulation models was attempting to link the projections of tourism growth to population projections through the labor force required for the additional jobs created. The official State population forecast showed that a growth rate midway between 5 percent and 10 percent growth in visitor arrivals would create the additional jobs matching the State's population forecast. With hindsight, the assumed rate of 5 percent growth in visitor arrivals was the closest to what happened. Hawaii had passed the rapid growth stage and was reaching the maturity stage during the 1980s, with an annual average increase in visitors of only 5 percent.

Returning to the net benefits of tourism to the public sector, the 1970 cost-benefit and 1978 public revenue-cost studies were not comparable due to more comprehensive data available for the 1978 study as well as differences in the classification of visitors used in the respective studies (Hawaii Office of Tourism 1978). The findings of the 1978 public revenue-cost study suggested:

- Public revenues received exceed public expenditures on visitors.
- Revenue cost ratios were smaller than in the 1970 study, however, this may have been due to differences in the data used.
- The higher the ratio of immigrants in the labor force attracted by tourism's growth, the lower the net benefits.
- Visitors who spend the most do not necessarily generate the highest public revenue-cost ratios.

- Revenue-cost ratios for visitors coming for conventions did not seem to differ much from those who did not come for a convention.
- Revenue-cost ratios for group travelers were higher than those for independent travelers.
- For group travelers, the revenue-cost ratios declined for repeat trips, but for independent travelers, the revenue-cost ratio increased for repeat trips.

The first three findings were consistent for both studies. The Mathematica study suggested that high-income visitors had slightly lower cost-benefit ratios than middle-income visitors. The 1978 study suggest that visitors with the highest expenditures per day do not necessarily have the highest public revenue-cost ratios. In addition, the 1978 study estimated that visitors in professional occupations who attended conventions had a public revenue-cost ratio that was slightly higher–3.98 versus 3.90–than visitors in professional occupations who did not come to attend a convention. On the other hand, visitors in nonprofessional occupations who attended a convention had a slightly lower public revenue-cost ratio–3.53 versus 3.61– than visitors in nonprofessional occupations who did not come to attend a convention (Hawaii Office of Tourism 1978, 63-67,98-99).

It is usually assumed that independent visitors are more beneficial to a destination than group visitors. The 1978 study estimated that the public revenue-cost ratios for group visitors were higher than those for independent travelers whether they were first time or repeat visitors. The public revenue-cost ratio for independent travelers did increase for repeat trips but still were not as high as for first time group travelers. The study's findings that visitors with high income, visitors that have high expenditures per day, convention visitors, and independent travelers do not necessarily have the highest public revenue-cost ratios are contrary to what people may think are the high-quality visitors to attract to Hawaii.

Following the State Tourism Study, a series of State Tourism Plans were completed and revised, and another Tourism Congress was held in 1984 (Hawaii Department of Planning and Economic Development 1985). A Tourism Impact Management System was established in 1986 to monitor and report on major tourism impact issues that needed to be addressed (Department of Business and Economic Development, Tourism Branch 1989). After Governor Waihee was elected in 1986, a major change in the State's organization occurred which affected land use and planning. Governor Waihee in 1987 transferred the State Office of Planning to be directly under the Governor's Office (State of Hawaii Office of Planning 2020). The State Office of Planning was responsible for reviewing the classification of all lands in the State and recommending changes to the LUC. From this date forward, recommending changes in land use classifications would be directly under the Governor's Office.

A second major change that affected the status of tourism within the State bureaucracy occurred two years later. The original State Tourism Office (STO) was created in 1976 by the Interim Tourism Policy Act. It was reorganized in 1984 as one of six branches in the Business and Industry Development Division of DPED. The STO's main function was to monitor the impact of tourism on the economic, social, and physical environment of Hawaii. The State legislature recognized the importance of tourism to Hawaii's economy and passed legislation to create a cabinet-level State

Office of Tourism, but Governor Waihee vetoed the legislation in 1989.

The Tourism Branch of the DPED was upgraded to the State Tourism Office (STO) in 1990 with a Deputy Director, and DPED was renamed the Department of Business, Economic Development & Tourism (DBEDT) (Hawaii State Archives 2002). It seemed that tourism was added on to the department's name to replace planning and as part of DBEDT's responsibility to foster business and economic development. The nature of subsequent plans by DBEDT adopted a business strategic planning approach in the form of a Strategic Marketing Plan for Tourism followed by a Strategic Tourism Plan.

The 1990s were a continuation of efforts to improve State tourism plans. A Tourism Functional Plan was developed in 1991 as part of the Hawaii State Functional Plans (State of Hawaii 1991). A Tourism Congress was held in 1993, followed by a mini-Congress in 1994. An interesting statement from the 1993 Tourism Congress Steering Committee was: "*The issues raised in this publication are not new; a report published in 1955 by the Hawaii Visitors Bureau and the Tourist Industry Committee highlighted similar critical issues facing Hawaii's visitor industry*" (Hawaii Visitors Bureau and Hawaii. Department of Business 1993, ii).

In partial response to the 1993 Tourism Congress recommendations, studies were completed on eco-tourism, health related tourism, and repositioning Hawaii's visitor industry products (Center for Tourism Policy Studies 1995). Up to this point in time, State Tourism Plans recognized the need to account for social and environmental impacts, but the focus seemed to remain on economic development. With the 1990s experience of instability and overall stagnation in visitor arrivals, there was an attempt to restructure and strengthen the State's organization responsible for tourism. The Hawaii Tourism Authority (HTA) was established in 1998 with a dedicated source of funding from the approval of a hotel room tax (Hawaii Tourism Authority 2020). Discussion of the HTA will be done in the next section on tourism promotion. Before leaving this section, the Hawaii Convention Center warrants some comment given its cost of $350 million to construct.

Other studies and recent articles already have shown that the Hawaii Convention Center has not been successful and after over two decades has not repaid $317 million in principal and interest for the project (Dayton 2016). It was known at the time of the market feasibility study in 1985 that Hawaii was at a disadvantage in bidding for major conventions, due to high costs for travel to Hawaii, travel time required and competition from other venues on the U.S. mainland. Most meetings and conventions had less than 5,000 delegates and the average attendance was less than 2,000 delegates. Hawaii already had the capacity to host most meetings and conventions with less than 5,000 delegates. The exceptionally large conventions of 5,000 or more are not necessarily the most lucrative and would likely be the most difficult to attract with numerous sites willing to compete by offering financing of pre-convention expenses incurred by sponsoring associations, as well as complimentary services to win the bid. Associations rely on profits from their conventions to supplement their budgets, which are otherwise funded primarily from membership dues. An association's selection of a site is based upon their expectation of a large attendance to generate maximum profits.

A *Washington Post* article reported in 1989 that a survey of 650 trade associations revealed that the average convention attendance decreased by 38 percent, to only 1,052, from 1986-1988. The number of seminar attendees declined by 25 percent to an average of 210 (Lawrence 1989). Seminar attendees responded that they preferred seminars because they were less expensive and closer to home. In addition to lower attendance and a preference for seminars closer to home, there was a decline in conventions and seminars since 1983. The site for the Hawaii Convention Center was not selected until 1993. In that same year, Hawaii experienced the sixth consecutive year of decline in meetings and conventions (Hawaii Visitors Bureau 1964, nos. 1988–1993). In view of the national trends of declining meetings and conventions and consecutive years of declines for Hawaii, it would seem difficult to justify moving forward on a project to construct a convention center, especially at a cost of $350 million. Nevertheless, the construction of the convention center was approved amidst some controversy (Rees 1993). The organization and funding of tourism promotion is discussed in the next section.

Tourism Promotion

The terms *marketing* and *promotion* are often used interchangeably, but as noted previously, promotion is only one of the variables encompassed by service marketing. Up until the formation of the HTA in 1998, the primary mandate of the HVB and its predecessors was to promote Hawaii. DPED had oversight of the HVB contract as one of its major responsibilities. The emphasis on tourism promotion by HVB was continued with the reorganization of DPED to DBEDT.

The promotion variables traditionally were advertising, personal selling, sales promotions, and publicity. HVB utilized all of the variables, some more effectively than others due to budget or other limitations. As discussed in previous chapters, books, movies and shows drew interest to Hawaii throughout the world. Local personalities as well as visiting dignitaries to the islands attracted attention to Hawaii, especially during the introduction and growth stages of Hawaii's tourism and probably had more impact on travelers' desires to visit Hawaii than HVB advertising. The introduction of jet travel and jumbo jets coupled with changes in CAB regulations made a vacation in Hawaii affordable to a broad segment of the population. This is not to say that HVB expenditures were not effectively used, since it only had modest funding ranging from $1.2 million in 1960 to $3 million in 1979. HVB expenditures, at best, had a nominal contribution to the success of Hawaii's tourism during the growth stages compared to the tourism promotion expenditures of the private sector and the effect of all the other factors fostering growth in travel to Hawaii.

After experiencing the first decline in visitors in 1980, HVB expenditures increased from $3.1 million in 1980 to $14.1 million in 1989 during the mature stage of Hawaii's tourism and continued to increase to $22.8 million in 1991 at the beginning of the stagnation stage. The slower growth of the mature stage and stagnation of the 1990s resulted from numerous external changes in world and national conditions that one would not expect could be overcome through increased promotional activity. In addition, the long-run effects of CAB deregulation negatively affected Hawaii's competitiveness, and the introduction of large passenger capacity, long-range aircraft resulted in Hawaii being overflown on more lucrative international routes.

HVB increasing promotion expenditures was the only short-run response to deteriorating industry conditions in Hawaii that it could do, since it did not have any control over the external factors negatively impacting Hawaii's tourism. The bi-annual budgeting and allocation of funding to the HVB from the State government was a barrier to long-term planning. State funding for the HVB at times has been a contentious issue due to State audits of expenditures as well as alternative uses that could be used with the funds allocated to the HVB during times of declining State revenues.

The original funding for tourism promotion in Hawaii was by the private sector through the Chamber of Commerce and Merchants' Association. Before the Second World War, funding for the Hawaii Tourism Bureau was primarily from the private sector with only one-third from government appropriations. The Territorial legislature agreed in 1949 to match private sector contributions on a 1:1 basis up to $250,000. The matching of funds continued over the next ten years even though total funding exceeded $500,000 (Hawaii Visitors & Convention Bureau 2020). The proportion of government funding increased from about 51 percent in 1959 to 93 percent in 1991. The State government was essentially providing all the HVB funding.

HVB expenditures remained modest, less than $3 million per year, up to 1978. Expenditures more than doubled to $8.6 million in 1987 and then almost tripled over the next four years to $22.8 million in 1991. It is difficult to understand the rationale for these extraordinary increases in expenditures within such a short time. The Hawaii economy was booming during the 1980s from the Japanese investments and increases in Japanese travelers due to the Plaza Accord, which devalued the U.S. dollar by almost 50 percent. Visitor arrivals increased by 15 percent in 1986 and continued to increase until 1990, reaching 6.7 million. The HVB expenditure increases from 1968-1990 was not in response to deteriorating industry conditions.

One might argue that the increase to $22.8 million in 1991 may have been in anticipation of potential negative effects of the Gulf War and the collapse of Japan's bubble economy, but these are the types of events that are not possible to forecast and promotional activity tend to have little effect on improving the situation. Despite the large increases in HVB expenditures, the number of visitor arrivals declined in 1991, which was the beginning of three successive years of decline in visitors. The 1990s was the stagnation stage for Hawaii's tourism.

The name of the HVB was changed in 1996 to the Hawaii Visitors & Convention Bureau (HVCB) to place emphasis on marketing to the meetings and conventions market as part of its responsibility to market the Hawaii Convention Center. The HTA was established in 1998 to create a strategic vision and direction for tourism and implement the key initiatives for sustainable, social, and economic benefits for all the islands of Hawaii (Hawaii Tourism Authority 2020). The HTA was to have dedicated funding from a Tourism Special Fund allocated from the Transient Accommodation Tax (TAT).

The TAT has been analyzed from different perspectives. From a public finance perspective there are three basic goals of taxation: 1) raise revenue to provide necessary government functions such as the provision of public goods; 2) redistribution function to reduce the unequal distribution of income and wealth that results from a market based economy; and 3) regulatory function to guide private sector activity (Avi-Yonah 2006). To clarify the first goal, a *public good* is a commodity or service that an individual can consume without reducing its supply, and no one can be excluded from using it (Musgrave 1959, 43–46; Pettinger 2019). An example of a *public good* would be national defense. Government provides other services such as public education based on being a *merit good*, i.e., it is so meritorious that the government should provide it to benefit everyone (Musgrave 1959, 13–14). Examples of quasi-public goods are roads and beaches, which have finite supply and could charge fees such as toll roads and membership for private beaches.

The progressive income personal income tax was originally conceived to redistribute income from higher income to lower income groups. The hotel room tax obviously was not imposed to redistribute income to reduce the unequal distribution of wealth. The regulatory function of a tax would be to discourage private sector activity that is detrimental to the public, such as the tax on cigarettes to discourage smoking. The hotel room tax was not imposed to discourage the use of hotels. In fact, there was concern that the room tax would discourage tourists from coming to Hawaii.

The TAT was enacted in 1986 as a tax on all transient accommodations, and up to 1990 all revenues from the tax went into the State General Fund. Beginning in 1991, the counties received a share of the tax revenues and in 1995 allocations were made to the Convention Center Fund. With the establishment of the HTA in 1998, revenues generated from the TAT were to be distributed as follows: Counties–44.8 percent; Tourism Special Fund–37.0 percent; Convention Center Enterprise Fund–17.3 percent and the State General Fund–0.9 percent. The tax rate has been increased five times throughout the years, from the original 5 percent in 1987 to the current rate of 10.25 percent. The distribution of the revenues also has changed throughout the years. Revenues from the TAT have increased from $168.6 million in 2000 to $600.3 million for Fiscal Year 2019.

A major reallocation of TAT revenues was done in 2015 to reflect the state and counties provision of public services (State of Hawaii Auditor and Belt Collins Hawaii LLC 2015). Almost three-fourths, 74 percent, of the total TAT revenues were allocated in 2019 to the State-$340 million and Counties-$103 million in line with their proportionate shares of providing public services. The legislature created special funds for mass transit which received $57.4 million, the Department of Land & Natural Resources received $3 million, and Turtle Bay to support land management initiatives on the North Shore received $1.5 million. The Tourism Special Fund, which is the funding for the HTA, received $79 million and the Convention Center received $16.5 million (Hawaii Tourism Authority 2019).

Allocations to the State, counties, and special funds for mass transit, DNLR and Turtle Bay were in line with funding public services from tax revenues. The question remains as to whether the Hawaii Convention Center and/or HTA meet the requirements of being *public goods or merit goods* to justify their funding by a tax. The Convention Center is clearly not a *public good* since its supply is finite and equivalent facilities are provided successfully by the private sector, which charges fees for their use. Considering the Convention Center as a *merit good* would be questionable since *merit goods* such as public education, healthcare, welfare services and fire protection provide services for the general population due to their beneficial effects on improving the welfare of society. In addition, it was estimated that the HTA had paid $455 million in principal and interest toward the debt for the Convention Center. The Center had lost $55.3 million since its opening and did not expect its first year of breaking even until 2018. Moreover, the Center still owed $297 million as of 2016 (Scharfers 2016).

Tourism promotion funded by the State government also is clearly not a *public good*, since its supply is finite, and the private sector spends more on tourism promotion than any government tourism bureau. During the early stages of Hawaii's tourism, one could argue that tourism was an infant industry that needed government support to develop because the existing private sector had inadequate resources. The ratio of 1:1 private sector funding to government funding seemed justified up to 1959. The infant industry argument cannot be used during the growth and maturity stages of Hawaii's tourism to justify the State government eventually funding all HVB tourism promotion when the tourism industry in Hawaii was well established and investing hundreds of millions of dollars on new resorts.

Developers were even willing to pay impact fees up to $100 million to develop golf courses for resorts.

The merits of the HTA, if any, would rely upon its ability to create a strategic vision and direction for tourism and implement the key initiatives for sustainable, social, and economic benefits for Hawaii. The HTA's first strategic plan in 1999 was Ke Kumu: Strategic Directions for Hawaii's Visitor Industry (Hawaii Tourism Authority 1999). The plan was based upon a competitive analysis and product assessment of Hawaii. The plan "*provided a policy directive towards 'sustainable tourism' by focusing on growing spending instead of measuring tourism's success by tracking arrivals*" (Hawaii Tourism Authority 2005, 1). Increasing spending may not have been the best way to achieve sustainable tourism. As indicated in the 1978 Public Revenue-Cost Analysis, visitors that spend the most do not necessarily generate the highest public revenue-cost ratios.

Ke Kumu was revised and approved two years later in 2002; and in 2003, HTA began revising the 2002 Ke Kumu (Hawaii Tourism Authority 2001; 2002). In addition to Ke Kumu, the Hawaii Tourism Strategic Plan (TSP) 2005–2015 was developed to provide a comprehensive plan to address the needs of all visitor industry stakeholders in Hawaii. The TSP was to serve as a guide for all stakeholders to work together towards the shared vision for Hawaii's tourism. HTA would continue to revise its own plan, Ke Kumu, in line with the TSP.

In 2016, the HTA developed a new five-year strategic plan. As background to the formation of the new plan, the HTA stated:

"In reality and from lessons learned in implementing TSP 2005-2015, the HTA does not have sufficient authority to enforce a 'State Plan', or to constantly monitor and oversee work done by other organizations. Therefore, this Strategic Plan is proposed as a dedicated 'HTA' plan that recognizes the need to work with partners and stakeholders for successful implementation." (Hawaii Tourism Authority 2016, 2–4).

The mission of the HTA was stated as:

"To strategically manage Hawaii's tourism in a sustainable manner consistent with economic goals, cultural values, preservation of natural resources, community desires, and visitor industry needs." (Hawaii Tourism Authority 2016, 2–4).

To achieve its mission, the HTA had four goals: 1) Improve the Integrity of the Destination; 2) Ensure Stable Economic Benefits; 3) Elevate Hawaii's Value Perception; 4) Strengthen HTA's Reputation (Hawaii Tourism Authority 2016, 2–4). The first goal is probably the most critical one in achieving the mission of the HTA since it recognized that *"a successful tourism economy balances the needs of the community, visitors and the destination."* The second goal to ensure stable economic benefits "*regardless of economic cycles or unforeseen events*" is beyond HTA's capabilities as was shown in the mature, stagnation and decline stages of Hawaii's tourism when increases in tourism promotion could not offset negative impacts from factors beyond HVB's control. Despite HTA's efforts, the stagnation and decline stages occurred from 1990-2009.

The third goal of elevating Hawaii's value perception is critical to Hawaii's competitiveness. Part of this goal was to maintain and improve air access to Hawaii. The HTA has no control over air access to Hawaii. In a deregulated environment, airlines will increase their capacity to match the demand for travel to Hawaii. A second part of this goal was to meet visitor expectations. The goal should not be to just meet visitor expectations but to exceed visitor expectations. Hawaii's brand must be earned through performance exceeding visitor expectations. The fourth goal is an outcome of HTA being successful in achieving its mission.

In 2019, the HTA started working on developing a new Strategic Plan 2020–2025. This was the first plan developed to reflect HTA's re-balancing from mainly marketing i.e., promotion to greater emphasis on destination management. The HTA's strategic direction was reorganized around four Pillars– Natural Resources, Hawaiian Culture, Community, and Brand Marketing (Hawaii Tourism Authority 2020, 26–28).

This was the first HTA Strategic Plan that established a high priority to providing services for both residents and visitors, to enhance the natural and cultural resources, support the native Hawaiian culture, and ensure that local communities benefit from tourism. The first three Pillars comprise the essence of Hawaii's brand and reflect the three additional service marketing variables that were missing in previous plans— people, both residents and tourists; process of delivering the experience; and physical evidence of Hawaii's unique cultures, diverse communities, and natural environment. By providing services to improve the welfare of the public, both residents and tourists, the HTA comes closer to being a *merit good* justified to be supported by the TAT. Otherwise, HTA and Convention Center funding from the TAT was simply a way for the State government to generate funds for tourism promotion and support the Convention Center by taxing tourists instead of using available public funds.

Summary

Early tourism plans had successful precedents to follow such as the land reclamation for Boston's Back Bay and Miami Beach, and the master planned resort community of Sea Pine Plantation on Hilton Head Island. Principles to guide the role of government in the development of Hawaii's Visitor Industry were outlined as key assumptions in the 1957 report by the Governor's Advisory Committee on the Tourist Industry. State actions throughout the years tended to focus on economic development. The private sector created plans to utilize lands for resort development and the State undertook studies to determine how to support visitor industry growth by providing infrastructure, programs, and facilities.

State of Hawaii government departments and State-funded tourism organizations seemed to respond to industry pressures on a reactive basis. Although several State Tourism Plans were developed throughout the years, follow through by the State government with the other management functions of organizing, leading, and controlling was lacking.

Although referred to as marketing, HVB and later HVCB throughout the years were primarily doing promotion. The same was true for HTA, with over three-fourths of the funds allocated to branding and less than one-fifth allocated to community programs. It was not until HTA's current 2020-2025 Strategic Plan that approximately one-third of the funds will be allocated to provide additional support for Hawaiian culture, natural resources, community activities and visitor safety. It may be necessary to allocate more HTA funds to community programs to achieve"*a successful tourism economy (that) balances the needs of the community, visitors and the destination* (Hawaii Tourism Authority 2020, 2).

Previous State tourism plans have not achieved a balance between the needs of the community and the visitor industry in Hawaii due to the focus on economic development. As early as 1983, Hawaii was seeking the quality visitor, which usually referred to high spending visitors. Attention also was being turned to Asia as well as the meetings, incentives, and convention markets. After thirty years, tourism promotional efforts have not been able to overcome external factors beyond the control of the State tourism organizations. Even the latest surge in visitors has not necessarily resulted in increased net benefits to the people of Hawaii, since real visitor expenditures have declined since 1989 despite increases in the number of visitors. Chapter 8 includes a discussion of the lessons learned from the past and their implications for the future.

Chapter 8

Past Lessons, Tourism Issues, Hawaii's Tourism in the Asia-Pacific Region

Overview

The global coronavirus pandemic placed the world into a holding pattern until the spread of the virus can be controlled. Economies are negatively affected by Covid regulations that have resulted in businesses closing and workers being laid off. Individuals and families have lower or no income due to layoffs. The travel industry has been one of the hardest hit industries with airlines, hotels, restaurants, and other hospitality related services losing billions of dollars. Returning to normal conditions will be dependent upon controlling the spread of the virus.

By placing activities on hold, the pandemic also provided an opportunity for evaluating the past and rethinking directions for the future. The time it will take to return to normal conditions is uncertain. Although vaccines have been developed for the original coronavirus, different strains of the virus have developed, and it is expected that the virus may continue to mutate similar to the flu. It may take several years to inoculate the world's population to reach a level of safety for the virus to be under control.

Flying to foreign destinations may be of lower priority for consumers compared to destinations closer to home and traveling by private automobile. The increased use of technology during the pandemic as a substitute for traveling for business, meetings, and personal gatherings have changed people's perspectives on alternatives to traveling. What were normal conditions prior to the pandemic will probably not be the same conditions in the future.

Compared to other parts of the United States and the world, Hawaii has been fortunate to have one of the lowest infection rates of the coronavirus and is considered a safer destination to visit compared to other destinations with high infection rates. Although international travelers are not allowed, U.S. travelers to Hawaii have rebounded rapidly during 2021 due to pent up demand and limited choice of destinations that are safe to visit. After experiencing a year with almost no tourists, residents are reacting negatively to the rapid growth in visitors causing congestion on roads, beaches, attractions, and other public places throughout the islands. Visitors are dissatisfied with the high prices, lack of rental cars, long-lines for restaurants and other facilities, and lower level of services due to Covid restrictions. A slower revival of Hawaii's tourism would have allowed more time to implement changes to work towards optimizing the growth of tourism for the benefit of both residents and tourists. Lessons based on past trends and experience may provide insights on future options for Hawaii's tourism.

Past Lessons

External Factors Beyond the Control of Hawaii

In his book, *Islands in Transition*, Thomas Hitch shares his insights on the development and transition of Hawaii's economy and lessons learned from Hawaii's experience. His first economic lesson from the past was: *"...it should suffice to demonstrate that most of the momentous changes that have taken place in the Hawaiian economy have been initiated by political, social, military, technological and other developments in other parts of the world, beyond the power of Hawaii to control"* (Hitch 1992, 249). This lesson applies to the development of tourism in Hawaii. Although the State government and private sector developed facilities to foster growth in tourism, the discussion in the previous chapters has shown that external factors such as improvements in transportation, wars in the Pacific, publicity on Hawaii through books, movies, shows, and Hawaiian performers, changes in CAB regulation, economic recessions, and technological innovations among other world-wide events have had more influence upon the pattern of growth of visitor arrivals than factors within the control of Hawaii.

Hawaii As the Crossroads of the Pacific–A Bygone Era

The establishment of Hawaii as the Crossroads of the Pacific has been an aspiration for decades. Hawaii initially had a geographical advantage as a stopover for transportation modes across the Pacific. Sailing ships were replaced by steamships; steamships by propeller airplanes; and propeller airplanes by jet airplanes. Eventually, long-distance aircraft made it possible and more profitable to overfly Hawaii than stopping over in the islands. Shipping routes from Asia travel directly to the major markets of the U.S. mainland, with goods then being transported from the U.S. mainland back to Hawaii. Unless there is a reason to stopover in Hawaii for expertise or resources only available in Hawaii, most transactions and activity across the Pacific bypass Hawaii. Innovations in technology have taken away any physical advantage of Hawaii being the Crossroads of the Pacific.

Hitch reviewed the ideas, organizations, and efforts to establish a role for Hawaii in the Pacific from the early 1900s Pan Pacific Union and Institute of Pacific Relations to the creation of the East-West Center or formally known as the Center for Technical and Cultural Exchange Between East and West (Hitch 1992, 300–307). Attempts to establish Hawaii as a regional Pacific headquarters for multinational corporations were not successful as exemplified by ITT Sheraton moving its regional Asia Pacific headquarters from Hawaii to Hong Kong. It was more efficient to have regional headquarters be in the major markets of Asia than in Hawaii.

Hitch identified two economic roles for Hawaii in the Pacific basin. The first was to continue to be the "most attractive place in the world for the people of the Pacific to visit for rejuvenation–not only vacationers...Perhaps most importantly, Hawaii is a place for the youth of the Pacific basin to gain an education" (Hitch 1992, 307). The second role was continuing to "serve as headquarters of the United States military in the half of the world that, stretching between the poles, encompasses the Pacific and Indian oceans." Hitch concludes his book with: "...the idea that there is some stellar economic role for Hawaii to play in the Pacific, other than in the fields of tourism and defense, is based more on hope than on reality" (Hitch 1992, 307).

Although thirty years have passed since Hitch's predictions, his conclusions on the role of Hawaii in the Pacific are still applicable today. Tourism and the military are the main sources of export income for Hawaii's economy. Efforts to diversify the economy have continued but have had limited success. Residents look toward the State government to diversify the economy. Government subsidies of industries typically do not work in the long-run and result in an inefficient allocation of resources. It is the private sector that must succeed in diversifying the economy. To do so, there must be a comparative advantage for an industry to locate in Hawaii to compete globally.

Diversifying Hawaii's economy

Regarding diversifying the Hawaiian economy, Hitch analyzed applicable industries to assess if Hawaii had any comparative advantages and potential industries to develop. Hitch's focus was on developing new exports or import replacement industries to diversify the Hawaiian economy. Based on his analysis, Hitch states: "*I conclude that the chances of the Hawaiian economy ever becoming largely diversified are nil*" (Hitch 1992, 300). On the other hand, Hitch felt that Hawaii's economy was "*moderately well diversified*" and not as narrowly concentrated as when Hawaii had little economic activity except sugar and pineapple. It should be noted that tourism was developed to diversify the economy when sugar and pineapple dominated the Hawaiian economy. Hitch's analysis covered the years up to his death in 1989. Like other island economies, Hawaii has limited natural resources to develop industries. Hawaii, furthermore, is located far from major markets.

The four major sources of income from export industries have been visitor expenditures, defense expenditures, sugar, and pineapple. Although federal government non-defense expenditures are not considered an industry, it has been a major source of external income to Hawaii. Data on Hawaii's balance of payments with the U.S. mainland and foreign countries are available only to 1978. Visitor expenditures, defense expenditures and federal government non-defense expenditures accounted for 78% of the funds coming from exports in 1978. Sugar and pineapple accounted for 10% and all remaining economic activity accounted for only 12% of the funds from exports (Bank of Hawaii Economics Division 1980, 29). Contrary to Hitch's predictions, sugar and pineapple have declined substantially since 1990. Visitor expenditures, defense expenditures and federal government non-defense expenditures have remained as the major sources of export income for Hawaii.

In terms of Gross State Product (GSP) or the total annual output of Hawaii, visitor expenditures accounted for 16.4 percent of GSP in 2017; defense expenditures accounted for 5.8 percent and federal government non-defense expenditures accounted for 5.0 percent (U.S. Bureau of Economic Analysis 2020). State and local government expenditures accounted for 9.2 percent of GSP. These four sectors accounted for over one-third, 36.4 percent, of GSP in 2017. Agriculture accounted for less than one percent, 0.5 percent, of GSP; manufacturing accounted for only 2 percent. As predicted by Hitch, the development of exports and import replacement industries would be limited in diversifying the Hawaiian economy. The Hawaiian economy is primarily a service-based economy. Services that could be exported to overseas organizations would be in the professional, educational, and scientific fields.

Tourism Issues

Diversifying Hawaii's Tourism

There have been numerous studies and attempts to diversify Hawaii's tourism. Studies to develop ecotourism, cultural tourism, health tourism, and agricultural tourism among others have had limited success, if any. Attempts to promote and increase visitors from specific market segments such as conventions, Europe and China have not been successful. Attracting the high-quality visitor has been elusive throughout the years with real visitor expenditures declining since 1989. Hitch's prediction that Hawaii's tourism would diversify and bring visitors for reasons other than rest and recreation have not materialized. Long-run trends have shown that the major markets and reason for visiting Hawaii have remained the same. The United States and Japan remain the major markets to Hawaii, and almost all visitors—85 percent— visit Hawaii for leisure purposes.

Long-run trends also showed that seven out of ten visitors are repeat visitors. A large proportion of repeat customers is usually a sign of success for a business. Repeat visitors have visited an average of seven trips to Hawaii so they exhibit high destination loyalty but are unlikely to repeat the same tourist activities that they did on their first trip, such as visiting tourist attractions, taking tours around the islands, going to luaus or Polynesian shows. Over their lifetime, repeat visitors will spend more in Hawaii than a first-time visitor so they are of substantial economic value to Hawaii. In addition, repeat visitors are information sources that link friends, relatives, and other potential travelers to a destination.

Quality of Tourism Employment

The tourism industry often is criticized as providing primarily low skill and low paying jobs. Hitch analyzed whether the perceived lower average wages of tourism workers was turning Hawaii into a low-income service economy. Hitch concluded that " T*he visitor industry is not turning Hawaii into a low-income economy. Whatever downward pull it has on average income in Hawaii is very small"* (Hitch 1992, 280). Hitch provided three reasons for his conclusion. First, with the multiplier effect, more than half of the employment related to visitor spending was in other sectors of the economy, where the wages would be equal to the average of non-visitor industry employees. Second, many of the jobs in the visitor industry, especially in food service, are part-time. Workers in these part-time positions typically work in more than one job so their annual earnings are not fully reflected by the earnings reported by the State Department of Labor. Third, many visitor industry workers receive tips, which could more than double their reported wages (Hitch 1992, 278–82).

A subsequent study utilized occupational data on Hawaii to examine whether jobs in tourism were primarily low skilled jobs and low paying. The data were for years that were included in Hitch's analysis. The perception that the tourist industry provides low-skill jobs relates to the disproportionate number of employees in service occupations in hotels and eating/drinking places (Choy 1995, 131). A significant proportion of these service positions, 25-30 percent, were in supervisory or skilled positions such as managers, professional and technical workers, bakers, chefs, and cooks.

The study revealed that the average annual wage in the airline industry was higher than the average annual wages for the government sector and the average annual wage for all industries, excluding government. The average annual wage for hotels was almost equal–85 percent– to that of all industries. Considering only service industries, the average annual hotel wage ranked fifth out of thirteen listed service industries. Only the average annual wage of legal services, engineering and management, health, and private education exceeded the annual average wage for hotels (Choy 1995, 133). The average annual wage for hotel workers were ranked relatively high even though approximately one-third of the jobs in hotels and lodging places were in service positions related to food service and another one-third in non-food service positions that tended to depress the average annual wage for hotels.

The average annual wage for eating and drinking places was only 50 percent of the average annual wage for all industries. As Hitch noted, many positions in eating and drinking places are part-time depending upon the hours of service. Workers in these part-time positions tend to have more than one job so their annual earnings are not fully reflected in earnings reported to the government. Foodservice workers also receive tips, which can double their wages. Furthermore, most of the service occupations in foodservice are part of eating and drinking places which serve residents, so one cannot conclude that the low wage in the foodservice industry is due only to the tourist industry.

The perception of low skills and low wages in the visitor industry is due to the nature of service occupations, especially in foodservice (Choy 1995, 132). People, who work outside of the industry, tend to have a more negative view of jobs in the industry, compared to those who work in the visitor industry (Choy 1995, 133). On the other hand, the people, who work outside of the industry with negative views of visitor industry jobs, expect a high level of service as airline passengers, hotel guests, restaurant patrons, and customers of tourist facilities when they travel. Many people, who work outside of the visitor industry, have lower average annual wages than those working in the visitor industry.

Although upward mobility in the visitor industry may be limited in Hawaii, aspiring executives and managers in the tourist industry have the opportunity to transfer worldwide to other properties and establishments within the corporate structures of the airlines and international chains. Hawaii residents have been successful as executives in the Asia-Pacific region as exemplified by Richard Hartman, who became the first president for ITT Sheraton's Asia-Pacific Division based in Hong Kong in 1985 (Chan 2020). It also can be noted that upward mobility in other sectors of the Hawaiian economy is limited by the number of executive positions available and is not a characteristic only of the visitor industry. Hawaii in general has limited opportunities for upward mobility due to the lack of large corporations compared to the U.S. mainland. As discussed in the next section, the quantity and quality of employment in visitor accommodations have changed due to structural changes in Hawaii's tourism industry.

Structural Changes in Hawaii's Tourism Industry

A major change in Hawaii's tourism industry has been the change in the ownership of hotels. Private equity firms including Blackstone Group, Cerberus Capital Management, Goldman Sachs, and MSD Capital have invested in hotel companies or individual hotel properties in Hawaii. A study in 2012 showed that private equity firms comprised five out of the top ten hotel owners by room count (Sadoski and Hou 2012, 6). The sale of Outrigger Hotels & Resorts in 2016 to Denver-based KSL Capital Partners meant that the majority of top hotel owners in Hawaii were financial companies (Schaefers 2020). Financialization of Hawaii's hotel industry has resulted in a focus on short-term profits and cost reduction. Studies on the financialization of other industries have shown that the focus on short-term profits has resulted in job losses (Rossman and Greenfield 2006). Similarly, there have been job losses in Hawaii's hotel industry due in part to financialization of the industry.

A second major change has been the shift towards developing timeshares, condotels, resort condominiums, and limited-service hotels instead of full-service hotels. This shift away from full-service hotels has resulted in lower employment requirements for the properties. The reduced services offered by the limited-service accommodations, in addition, changed the nature of employment toward primarily service occupations for cleaning and maintenance of the properties.

A third major change has been the proliferation of illegal vacation rentals, which has resulted in the loss of tax revenues in addition to lowering income and employment effects of increases in visitor arrivals. Like limited-service accommodations, vacation rentals generate mostly service occupations for cleaning and maintenance of the rentals. The income gained from illegal vacation rentals is at the expense of legal establishments as well as residents who indirectly are subsidizing the illegal vacation rentals. If owners of illegal vacation rentals are not paying required federal, state and city taxes, then the cost of providing public services to illegal vacation rentals are not being recovered from the rents paid by visitors staying in the illegal vacation properties. From a public sector viewpoint, the public revenue-cost ratios for visitors staying in illegal vacation rentals are likely to be negative. Owners of illegal vacation rentals also may be liable for tax fraud.

The shift away from full-service hotels has resulted in a change in the relationship between increases in the number of visitor arrivals and the benefits generated in terms of income and employment. When out-of-state owners of illegal vacation rentals transfer their profits out of Hawaii, this would result in a loss of income to Hawaii. Illegal vacation rentals, moreover, have resulted in less housing available for residents to rent or buy.

Residents' Attitudes Toward Tourism

As part of the Tourism Impact Management System, a Statewide Tourism Impact Core Survey was conducted to develop information on tourism's impacts on Hawaii. Residents were asked their opinion on whether "*Tourism has brought more benefits than problems.*" The Core Survey was to be conducted on a two- or four-year cycle in line with the review processes for County and State Plans. In 1988, the first year of the survey, 75 percent of respondents strongly agreed or somewhat agreed that tourism brought more benefits than problems (Community Resources 1989, iii). Agreement with the statement reached a high of 80 percent in 2010 and declined to a low of 58 percent in 2019 ("Resident-Sentiment-Board-Presentation-02-27-20.PDF"). The biggest decline was for respondents who completely agreed with the statement. In 2010, 45 percent of respondents completely agreed that tourism brought more benefits than problems (OmniTrak Group Inc. 2011). Strong support for tourism, i.e., those who completely agreed, declined throughout the last decade by more than half to only 19 percent in 2019.

For residents responding that tourism creates more problems than benefits, traffic was selected by 68 percent of respondents as a major problem. Higher cost of living, overcrowding, and damage to the environment were selected by 63 percent of respondents as problems created by tourism. No respect for culture and traditions was selected by 57 percent of respondents and too dependent on tourism by 47 percent of respondents ("Resident-Sentiment-Board-Presentation-02-27-20.PDF"). These problems have persisted throughout the years, and the substantial increases in visitor arrivals during the recovery stage have exacerbated the problems.

Independent research on whether perceived tourism impacts increased the likelihood of tourism-related stress was conducted using a sample of residents of Oahu. The top five tourism impacts were traffic, crowding and congestion, my personal life quality, respect for my way of life, and peace and quiet.

Additional insights were gained from the responses such as:

"... having to deal with ... the large vehicles and tourists driving cars in the area and tourists on bikes.

"Crowded shopping centers...crowded beaches and hiking trails overrun by tourists."

"Taking my children to school and other activities takes three times as long!"

"No respect for our laws. No information given before arrival as to laws and culture. VERY RUDE." (Jordan, Lesar, and Spencer 2019, 6–7).

The research discovered five other issues that emerged from the responses: vacation rentals, diffusion of visitor flows, governance, overuse of natural resources, and general economic impacts. The vacation rental issue related to the disturbances caused by vacation rentals as well as their illegality are reflected in the response:

"Vacation home renters blowing a conch shell to greet the morning sun, cursing at the neighbors, tossing trash into the streets, blasting the stereo 12 hours straight, hollering as though they are in Waikiki, etc." (Jordan, Lesar, and Spencer 2019, 7).

The diffusion of visitor flows was related to visitors going into areas that previously were not frequented by visitors. The governance issue was related to the perceived lack of government efforts to manage tourist activities and growth. The overuse of natural resources is similar to the Core Survey problem of damage to the environment. General economic impacts were related to impacts in specific areas such as day trippers to Kailua. The tourism impacts and issues identified in the independent research reflected recent changes such as the growth in vacation rentals and diffusion of visitors, which the Core Survey does not capture due to the generic nature of the Core Survey questions.

Hawaii's Tourism in the Asia-Pacific Region

Historically, the three most well-known islands for tourism in the Asia-Pacific region were Tahiti, Bali, and Hawaii. Tahiti formed the image of a Pacific Island paradise as expressed in the paintings of Tahitian landscapes and natives by the famous French artist, Paul Gauguin, who lived and painted in Tahiti and the Marquesas Islands from 1891 until his death in 1903 (Biography.com 2020). Gauguin's paintings were not recognized until after his death and became the basis for the Primitivism art movement of the early 1900s. The movie, Mutiny on the Bounty, showed the beauty of Tahiti as the mutiny occurred when the ship stopped over in Tahiti, which today is part of French Polynesia, a territory of France (Editors 2021).

Bali was first recognized as a tropical paradise by the Dutch, who had colonized Indonesia. What Gauguin found in Tahiti, Dutch as well as other European travelers in the early 1900s found in Bali, where the native culture and arts were still preserved, compared to Tahiti where the native population had been converted to Christianity. Bali attracted artists, writers, scholars, and musicians from around the world, who popularized the culture and beauty of the island. The famous anthropologist Margaret Mead described the Balinese culture as being relatively untouched and adapting to foreign influence (Awani Bali 2018.)

After WWII, Hawaii grew to be the most popular destination in the Asia-Pacific region up until 1994, when Asian destinations began to dominate. In 2018, Hawaii received 9.7 million visitors. Of the total number of visitors, 6.7 million were visitors from the U.S. mainland and 3.0 million were international visitors (Hawaii Tourism Authority 2019). Given the distance of Hawaii from the U.S. mainland, domestic U.S. visitors to Hawaii are comparable to long-haul international visitors to other destinations. The total number of visitors to Hawaii in 2018 was more than any other destination in Oceania.

Australia received 9.2 million international visitors and New Zealand only received 3.7 million international visitors in 2018. The other eighteen Pacific islands received less than one million international visitors, except for Guam with 1.5 million international visitors. The next most popular Pacific Island destination was Fiji with 900,00 international visitors. The total number of international visitors to Oceania in 2018 was 16.9 million (United Nations World Tourism Organization 2020). Excluding Australia, New Zealand, and Hawaii, the eighteen Pacific islands in Oceania together received only four million international visitors, which was less than half of the total visitors to Hawaii.

Hawaii also compared favorably to Asian destinations. Of the twenty-two independent, Asian destinations included in UNWTO data, Hawaii would rank as the eleventh most popular destination in 2018. The number of visitors to Hawaii exceeded that of the Philippines, Cambodia, Laos, and less popular Asian destinations. The top five most popular Asian destinations were China, including Hong Kong and Macau with 110.7 million international visitors; Thailand with 38.2 million; Japan with 31.2 million; Malaysia with 25.8 million and India with 17.4 million international visitors (United Nations World Tourism Organization 2020). The growth of visitors to these destinations increased during the late 1980s and throughout the 1990s.

Considering the geographical isolation of the Hawaiian Islands, its prominence as a leisure destination in the Asia-Pacific region would not have occurred without the economic, political, and social ties to the United States. French Polynesia has islands as beautiful as the Hawaiian Islands, relatively untouched by major development compared to Hawaii. The Tahitian culture and people are very hospitable and welcoming. The second wave of settlers to Hawaii, in fact, came from the Marquesas Islands, which are part of French Polynesia. Distance from major markets and high travel costs, however, has limited Tahiti's tourism to only 216,300 visitors in 2018 (World Bank 2019).

Bali is located close to major markets within Asia and Oceania and was a popular overseas destination for Australians. Bali's arts, performances and culture are major attractions in addition to its beaches, which are popular with surfers. Bali today is the most popular attraction in Indonesia with six million visitors in 2018 compared to Hawaii's over nine million visitors in the same year (Woods 2020; Hawaii Tourism Authority 2019). No Pacific Island has been as successful as Hawaii in developing its tourism, and Hawaii receives more visitors than many countries in Asia. The coronavirus pandemic, however, has made it difficult to predict what may happen in the future. The last chapter discusses actions that can be taken in facing an uncertain future.

Chapter 9
Uncertain Future

At the time that this book was written, it was impossible to predict as to how and when worldwide travel would recover from the global pandemic. The severity and duration of the impact of the global pandemic upon people's lives had not been experienced before. Although it is expected that travel will eventually return to normal levels, there is no clear picture of what normal levels will be. Individuals' way of life changed dramatically during the pandemic, and their post-pandemic behavior would be expected to change due to the financial, social, physical and psychological impacts of the pandemic.

On a positive note, the pandemic has provided an extended pause in tourist activities so that a new beginning for tourism in Hawaii can be envisioned. Although complete sustainability is impossible to achieve, the tourism industry can work towards achieving sustainability goals and reducing the negative impacts of tourism. A shift toward prioritizing residents' needs is needed to balance the needs of residents versus the activities of visitors. Tourism should be used to generate benefits for residents and as a basis for diversifying the economy. Possible ways to achieve these objectives are discussed in this chapter.

Sustainable Tourism

Except for resident attitudes, the negative impacts of tourism upon Hawaii have not been discussed in order to deal with negative impacts within the context of working towards sustainability not only for the tourism industry but also for Hawaii overall. A beginning point would be to consider the goals of sustainable tourism. The UNWTO's definition of sustainable tourism development is:

"Tourism that takes full account of its current and future economic, social and environmental impacts, addressing the needs of visitors, the industry, the environment and host communities." Thus, sustainable tourism should:

1. Make optimal use of environmental resources that constitute a key element in tourism development, maintaining essential ecological processes and helping to conserve natural heritage and biodiversity.
2. Respect the socio-cultural authenticity of host communities, conserve their built and living cultural heritage and traditional values, and contribute to inter-cultural understanding and tolerance.
3. Ensure viable, long-term economic operations, providing socio-economic benefits to all stakeholders that are fairly distributed, including stable employment and income-earning opportunities and social services to host communities, and contributing to poverty alleviation" (UNWTO 2020).

As discussed in Chapter 7, the basic tenet of sustainable tourism development goes at least as far back as 1956, when Charles Fraser wanted to design a resort that respected the environment

(Retire Hilton Head .com 2020; The Cultural Landscape Foundation 2020). The concept of sustainable tourism has been discussed for decades, but progress towards achieving sustainability has been elusive. A sustainable approach for tourism is complex to design because activities related to tourism affect almost all aspects of a destination directly or indirectly. Recent advances have resulted in the development of approaches, programs, and quality control tools for progressing towards sustainability through the monitoring and management of the tourism industry (Lesar, Weaver, and Gardiner 2020). Adopting policies, programs, and activities to monitor, refocus and adapt Hawaii's tourism toward becoming more sustainable are part of destination management, which is discussed next.

Destination Management

Destination management can be taken in the context of the private sector where destination management companies (DMC) are vendors that handle the local arrangements at a destination for out-of-town organizations planning to have an event or special activities at a destination. In the public sector, a destination management organization (DMO) takes on a broader role as described by the UNWTO:

"Destination management consists of the coordinated management of all the elements that make up a tourism destination... Destination management calls for a coalition of many organizations and interests working towards a common goal, ultimately being the assurance of the competitiveness and sustainability of the tourism destination... From a traditionally marketing and promotion focus the trend is to become leading organizations with a broader mandate which includes strategic planning, coordination and management of activities within an adequate governance structure with the integration of different stakeholders operating in the destination under a common goal" (UNWTO 2020).

The HTA was established to take on a broader role than tourism promotion. However, the HTA relinquished its role of destination management after the TSP 2005-2015 and developed a new plan dedicated to the HTA predominately focusing on promotion. Under new leadership, the HTA's Strategic Plan 2020-2025 reflected a re-balancing of funds between promotion versus destination management. Promotional funds or Branding declined from 75.4 percent of HTA funds in 2017 to 60.7 percent budgeted for 2020. Funds for Community Programs increased from 16.6 percent in 2017 to 32.4 percent budgeted for 2020 (Hawaii Tourism Authority 2020, 12).

The coronavirus pandemic is not a situation where promotional efforts are effective. Hawaii already is well-known throughout the world. Travelers today depend upon destination websites, social media, and other online sources in selecting which destination to visit for the activities they want to do. There needs to be structural changes in managing Hawaii as a destination. Promotional efforts should be left to the private sector. For the government, the focus should shift from promotion to managing the factors that are within the control of Hawaii to improve Hawaii as a destination. At this stage of the product life cycle, product improvement to enhance the experience of both residents and visitors is a more effective strategy than continuing to do the government funded promotional activities that were done in the past.

HTA should be reorganized to focus on destination management and work toward sustainable goals. The allocation of HTA funds should be reversed to prioritize destination management. That is, 65 percent of the HTA funds should be allocated to work towards reducing the negative impacts of tourism and improving Hawaii for both residents and visitors to enjoy. The remaining 35 percent would be allocated for other activities to be done by the Hawaii Visitors Bureau, Hawaii Convention Center, and the four island visitor bureaus.

HTA's research activities are based upon the data collected by DBEDT. It would be sensible to consolidate HTA's research activities under DBEDT to avoid duplication of activities. HTA's and HVCB's responsibility to promote conventions should be shifted to the Hawaii Convention Center. In this way, there will be one organization accountable for conventions. The responsibility for continued development and maintenance of Hawaii's destination website would be the responsibility of the renamed Hawaii Visitors Bureau, which would focus on improving the visitor experience in their trip planning and during their stay in Hawaii by providing up-to-date information on Hawaii and expanding services to visitors in trip planning and during their stay in Hawaii.

Each island visitor bureau would receive funds directly for managing and improving tourism for their respective islands. Visitors to each island differ significantly such that general branding does not serve each island equally. For example, the Japanese market tends to visit Oahu with only limited visits to the other islands. Promoting the Hawaii Convention Center for the most part benefits Oahu. An important underlying rational in restructuring the government funded tourism organizations is to reduce administrative costs by eliminating the layers of overhead costs and focusing the efforts of each organization to improve their respective effectiveness and accountability. An additional benefit is that most of the funds will be spent in Hawaii, generating additional income and employment for residents.

In restructuring State–funded tourism organizations, the purpose and use of the Hawaii Convention Center also should be re-evaluated. Since 1990, the number of convention visitors have declined despite the construction of the Hawaii Convention Center. The benefits to the State government from convention visitors do not necessarily exceed that of other visitors, since the public revenue-cost ratios of convention visitors did not differ much from those of visitors not coming for conventions. The Convention Center should serve the needs of the general public to move towards becoming a *merit good* to justify its funding by taxes. A study should be done to analyze whether it would be beneficial to repurpose the Convention Center to generate additional funds and/or serve the general public.

Thus, the restructuring of State–funded tourism organizations would result in:

- HTA focusing on destination management to reduce negative impacts of tourism, improve Hawaii for residents and visitors to enjoy, and work towards achieving sustainability goals for Hawaii.
- HVCB renamed to HVB focusing on development and maintenance of Hawaii's destination website and

improving visitors' experiences in their trip planning and during their stay in Hawaii.

- Hawaii Convention Center focusing on the marketing and operations of the Convention Center.
- Direct funding to the four island visitor bureaus, i.e., Oahu Visitor Bureau, Maui Visitor Bureau, Kauai Visitor Bureau, and Big Island Visitor Bureau, to focus on managing and marketing tourism for their respective islands.
- DBEDT assuming HTA research activities.
- Conducting an independent re-evaluation of the purpose and use of the facilities of the Hawaii Convention Center.
- Allocating 65 percent of HTA's funds to destination management, with the remaining 35 percent allocated to accomplish the other activities.

Using Tourism to Diversify Hawaii's Economy

People's opinion that the State must diversify for the sake of diversification, so as not to be dependent only on one industry is an outdated concept. Corporations discovered that diversifying into other fields to achieve growth and minimize dependency on one business was not successful. A five-year study of 1,850 companies revealed that sustained, profitable growth was achieved when a company pushes out the boundaries of its core business into adjacent space, i.e., diversify into fields related to its core business (Zook and Allen 2003). Similarly, Hawaii should be looking to using the expertise from tourism as a means to discovering related areas for diversification. For example, Hawaii has planning and architectural companies that are world renown for their expertise in planning and designing resorts.

Professional Opportunities Provided by Tourism

Belt Collins was established in 1953. It was the first professional planning company in the Asia-Pacific region to combine urban and land planning, civil engineering, landscape architecture and environmental consulting within one professional organization. The company has overseas offices in Hong Kong, Shenzhen, Vietnam, Philippines, and Guam. The company employs over 500 professional and support staff and has completed projects in over 70 countries and territories throughout the world. Belt Collins consistently ranks among the top international design firms and top U.S.–based design firms (Belt Collins Hawaii 2020).

Wimberly, Whisenand, Allison, Tong & Goo was established in 1971. The history of the firm began in 1945 when George "Pete" Wimberly formed Wimberly and Cook in Honolulu. The company handled the renovation of the Royal Hawaiian Hotel in 1946; expanded to the South Pacific in designing the Hotel Tahiti in 1958; and redefined resort design with the opening in 1961 of the Hotel Bora Bora with guest rooms over the water. The name was changed to Wimberly, Allison, Tong & Goo in 1988 (Wimberly, Allison, Tong & Goo 2020, 1–2). With its main offices in Honolulu, the company opened offices in Cairo, Dubai, Irvine CA, London, Los Angeles, New York, Shanghai and Singapore. In addition, the company has satellite offices in other regions, including New Delhi and Istanbul. The company's projects range from hotel and resorts in China, Mexico and the Maldives, to the Venetian Resort, Encore and Wynn Resort in Las Vegas, to the St. Regis Hotel and Residences in Singapore (Wimberly, Allison, Tong & Goo 2020, 3–6).

Other professional service companies had offices in Hawaii during the growth stage of Hawaii's tourism. Harris, Kerr, Foster, now known as PKF (Pannell, Kerr, Foster) was the first company offering specialized consulting and benchmark services for the hospitality industry (PKF hotelexperts group 2020). Peat, Marwick, Mitchell, now known as KPMG also provided consulting and professional services for the hospitality industry in Hawaii and expanded to Asia (Richter 1986). Although positions in Hawaii may be limited, these professional, planning, architectural and consulting companies provide worldwide opportunities for Hawaii residents and graduates of the University of Hawaii with specialties such as urban & regional planning, engineering, architecture, environmental management and travel industry management among others.

Numerous professional jobs related to tourism are available but often not recognized by the public, who typically associate tourism jobs with the direct providers of services such as the airlines, hotels, travel agents, ground transportation and other hospitality operations. Support services or indirect providers such as destination management companies, marketing companies, advertising agencies, travel publications, tour wholesalers and event organizers provide professional opportunities. Organizations that are involved in the development of tourism such as planning companies, architecture companies, government agencies, financial companies, real estate developers and educational institutes provide opportunities that require some of the highest levels of professional skills. The professional skills required for tourism development goes far beyond the management of tourist facilities. Providing tourism education and training for students and professionals within the Asia-Pacific region can be a means to establish a role for Hawaii in the Pacific and diversify the economy as a center for tourism education and training.

Hawaii as a Center for Tourism Education and Training

The first economic role in the Pacific that Hitch identified for Hawaii was to continue to be "the most attractive place in the world for the people of the Pacific to visit." As part of that role, Hitch noted: "Perhaps most importantly, Hawaii is a place for the youth of the Pacific basin to gain an education" (Hitch 1992, 307). The beginnings of the University of Hawaii date back to 1907 as a land grant College of Agriculture and Mechanic Arts. The College became a university in 1920. An Oriental Institute was established in 1935 (University of Hawaii at Manoa 2020). The Pacific Islands Studies Program at the University of Hawaii dates to 1950. Activities during the early years of the Pacific Islands Studies Program were typically limited to interests and projects in tropical agriculture by university faculty and scientists of the Bishop Museum. The program did not have any dedicated faculty, finances, or other resources until 1978 (Center for Pacific Islands Studies 2020).

In 1955, the Church College of Hawaii established higher education facilities to provide education to students from the Pacific Basin (Cook 2020). The activities of the Church College were extended when it developed the Polynesian Cultural Center (PCC) in 1963 to provide authentic displays of the different cultures existing throughout Polynesia from the Maoris in New Zealand to Tahitians, Samoans and other islands (Polynesian Culture Center 2020). The PCC, in an entertaining way, introduced millions of tourists and residents to the cultures of the Pacific Islands. Since its opening in 1963, over 37 million people have visited the PCC. An underlying reason for developing the Center was to provide employment for the Pacific Island students attending the College. Through their work at the Center, the students gained expertise in tourism operations that they took with them when they returned to their homes. In 1974, the Church College was renamed Brigham Young University (BYU) Hawaii (Brigham Young University 2020).

At the Federal government level, the seeds of recognizing Hawaii as a center for cultural exchange and education were planted when President Eisenhower in 1960 authorized the creation of a Center for Cultural and Technical Interchange between East and West in Hawaii (East West Center 2009). The East-West Center (EWC) was established as a national educational institution to foster better relations and understanding between the United States and countries in the Asia-Pacific region. The EWC was located in Hawaii because Congress and the U.S. Department of State felt that Hawaii offered special advantages for a national institution with an Asia-Pacific focus that could not be duplicated anywhere else in the country. The Center was linked to the University of Hawaii and located on its Manoa Campus. The EWC established the Pacific Islands Development Program (PIDP) in 1980 (Pacific Islands Development Program 2020a). The Pacific Islands Tourism Professional Fellows Program was started in 2018 to bring tourism industry professionals from Pacific islands for an intensive six-week program in Honolulu (Pacific Islands Development Program 2020b).

From a regional tourism perspective, the First Pacific Area Travel Conference was held in Honolulu from January 12-15, 1952. The conference initially was organized through the efforts of Lorrin Thurston, publisher of the Honolulu Advertiser and William Mullahey of Pan American World Airways (Gee, Lurie, and Pacific Asia Travel Association 2001, 1–3). Invitations were sent to governments and transportation companies. The first conference resulted in the formation of the Pacific Interim Travel Association which at the second conference in 1953 was made permanent as the Pacific Area Travel Association (PATA) with headquarters in San Francisco. The establishment of PATA marked the beginning of promoting travel to the Asia-Pacific region through cooperative efforts of governments to facilitate travel to the region, and promotional efforts by PATA (Gee, Lurie, and Pacific Asia Travel Association 2001, 12–13, 27).

The U.S. Department of Commerce and PATA contracted Checchi and Company in 1961 to produce a report on The Future of Tourism in the Pacific and Far East (Clement 1961). The report was done to assist the countries in the region in developing tourism to enhance their economic development. In the same year, the idea of establishing a higher education program to support the growing tourism expected for the Asia-Pacific region was discussed at PATA's Ninth Annual Conference held in New Zealand. Through the efforts of William Mullahey of Pan American World Airways and Hawaii's Governor William Quinn, serving as PATA president, the University of Hawaii approved in 1962 a Department of Hotel & Tourism Management in the College of Business Administration (School of Travel Industry Management 2006, 20–21). The department formed the basis for the School of Travel Industry Management (TIM), which was approved in 1966. Under the leadership of Dr. Edward M. Barnet, the TIM School diverged from the traditional model of a hotel school and encompassed the fields of transportation, hotel, and tourism management. Dr. Barnet coined the term, "travel industry management" to reflect the fact that all three areas comprised the core of the travel industry and are interrelated (School of Travel Industry Management 2006, 21–22). This was a step toward developing Hawaii as a center for tourism education and training for the Asia-Pacific region.

Despite limited resources and faculty, the TIM School had a major impact in educating hundreds of domestic and international students as well as professionals from throughout the Asia-Pacific region. In addition to its undergraduate and graduate degree programs, the TIM School established the Executive Development Institute for Tourism (EDIT) Program in 1979 (School of Travel Industry Management 2006, 56). EDIT was attended throughout the years by over 500 tourism professionals from over fifty countries around the world. The School's Office of Professional Programs offered custom designed programs and has worked with various governments, including a major training program for the staff of the Abu Dhabi Tourism Administration in the Middle East. TIM faculty, moreover, conducted numerous executive seminars and training workshops throughout the Asia-Pacific region.

When China opened its doors to tourists, the TIM School was the first to provide training during the 1980s for staff of the major tourism companies under the China National Tourism Organization of the People's Republic of China. A Professional Program for Tourism Studies (PPTS) was developed through private funding to bring tourism professionals from China to study one-year at the TIM School. PPTS participants returned to China to assist in the early development of China's tourism industry and assumed leadership positions. One of the PPTS participants rose through the ranks of China International Travel Service and became the Chairman of the Board of Directors for one of China's largest State travel companies.

Research grants by the TIM School have encompassed tourism manpower development for the American Pacific Islands funded through the Pacific Business Center under a grant from the U.S. Economic Development Administration, and tourism development studies of ten Pacific Island countries funded by the EWC Pacific Island Development Program (University of Hawaii at Manoa. School of Travel Industry Management and Pacific Basin Development Council 1983; Center for Tourism Policy Studies 1987). During the 1980s and into the 1990s the TIM School was the Center for Tourism Education and Training in the Asia-Pacific region. The TIM School accomplished more than what would be expected from its relatively small budget and faculty resources. An Associate Dean of the well-known Cornell School of Hotel Administration once confided that Cornell wished it had the reputation of the TIM School in the Asia-Pacific region.

The TIM School is a successful example of diversifying from tourism into professional education and training, both within Hawaii and throughout the Asia-Pacific region. Key elements to expand activities to further develop Hawaii as a Center for Tourism Education and Training exist in terms of the professional and educational organizations already located in Hawaii.

Economic Linkages to Tourism

Economists refer to the multiplier effect of tourist expenditures generating income and employment through the direct, indirect, and induced effects. The emphasis often is placed upon direct tourism expenditures as in the quest for high quality, higher spending tourists. The proportion of expenditures that comprise imported goods and services, however, can substantially reduce the multiplier effects especially in the case of island economies where most of the goods are imported from other areas. In island economies with limited productive capacity, the multiplier effect can be less than one. That is, a dollar of tourist expenditures generates less than a dollar of income in the local economy due to the large proportion of imports required to provide the goods and services consumed by tourists. The degree of importation can be reduced if tourist expenditures are linked to the production of a local economy.

The Hawaii Regional Cuisine movement was started in 1991 by twelve chefs in Hawaii to create dishes based upon the products grown in Hawaii and that reflect the various cultures to develop Hawaii as a culinary destination (Yamashita 2020). Many of the chefs worked at hotels or other establishments serving visitors and already had created dishes with fresh ingredients from the islands. The intent was for chefs to work with a network of local farms and ranches to provide the food products for their dishes. At the time, the chefs were developing backward linkages to local food producers. This is similar to the current farm to table movement in the foodservice industry. By developing a cuisine distinctive to Hawaii using local products, the chefs went from the table to the farm.

Other products that can be linked to Hawaii's tourism would be artwork, woodwork and customized products of local artists, designers, and artisans to be used in the decor, uniforms and supplies for tourist–related operations as well as being available for purchase. An international example would be the Regent Hotel of Manila, which used local rattan for its furniture and elevated rattan furniture to be used in a luxury setting. The rattan industry boomed in the Philippines but was limited by the supply of natural abaca strands from which real rattan is made. Another international example was The Manila Hotel with carved desks made of local woods in each room that guests could purchase and have shipped to their homes. Hawaii already has many local products that are used as part of a company's branding and part of a guest's experience. Developing new local products to fit the requirements of tourist businesses and expanding the use of local products in tourist businesses, not only in Hawaii but also worldwide, would create new opportunities for local entrepreneurs.

The story of local family business, ABC Store, is one of entrepreneurship diversifying from the resident market to tourists (Reference for Business 2020). Sidney Kosasa was trained as a pharmacist and opened Kaimuki Pharmacy in 1949. He then opened the Medical Arts Pharmacy in 1954, followed by Thrifty Drug of Hawaii with five stores. From a trip to Miami, Kosasa saw the opportunity of opening convenience stores for tourists as an alternative to high priced hotel shops. He opened the first ABC Discount Store in Waikiki in 1964 and purchased a grocery store in 1968. Prescription drugs and a pharmacist eventually were eliminated from the stores. Alcohol, touristy gifts, and other convenience items for tourists were added, and the name was shortened to ABC Store. The chain's expansion throughout Waikiki, the neighbor Islands, Guam, Saipan, and Las Vegas is well-known.

Paul Kosasa succeeded his father as president of the company in 1999. Under Paul's leadership, the company diversified into opening a high-end grocery store in Waikoloa in 2001. In addition to groceries, Island Gourmet Markets had a full-service deli, bakery, and wine bar with appetizers. Additional Island Gourmet Markets were opened in resorts on other islands. One of the largest investments, Duke's Lane Market & Eatery opened in 2017 with a full-service restaurant in addition to a deli, bakery, burger bar, various dessert, wine, and drinks bars, as well as gourmet foods (Taketa 2017). The full-service restaurant, Basalt, is popular with both residents and tourists due to its locally based cuisine and free parking for three hours. In its own way, Basalt was bringing residents back to Waikiki. The story of ABC Store diversifying from a pharmacy serving residents to a chain of convenience stores serving tourists, to a chain of gourmet marketplaces, and to a full-service restaurant serving both residents and tourists is an excellent example of using tourism to diversify into related fields. One also should note that ABC Store is one of the largest sellers of locally made products to tourists. Its foodservice operations and gourmet marketplaces, furthermore, use locally sourced products to the extent possible.

Whether backward linkages from tourists to locally produced goods and services, or moving into related fields, tourism provides opportunities to diversify Hawaii's economy and increase the income and employment benefits of tourist expenditures by reducing the import content of tourist expenditures. The linkages, more so, provide opportunities for local entrepreneurs to develop new businesses and create opportunities in Hawaii and abroad.

Moving Forward Toward an Uncertain Future

Under conditions of uncertainty, different strategies must be adopted in moving forward. There are different conditions of uncertainty ranging from a clear enough future where a single forecast is sufficient to determine strategy to true ambiguity where there is no basis to forecast the future (Courtney, Kirkland, and Viguerie 1997). The Covid-19 pandemic has produced a condition of true ambiguity about the future. Under these conditions, Hawaii can take a leadership position in shaping the tourism industry to progress towards sustainability for Hawaii as a whole and not just for the industry, itself. This approach goes beyond developing a sustainable tourism industry and looks towards using tourism as a contributor to the sustainability of the area (Moscardo 2008).

Tourism can contribute to an area's sustainability through product synergies, market synergies and marketing synergies (Moscardo 2008, 7–8). Product synergies refer to the shared use of resources. Kahuku Farms is an example of product synergies where a company with four generations of farmers growing local produce expanded into farm tours, a cafe, and producing over a dozen farm-based products ranging from lilikoi butter to hand soaps that are popular with both residents and tourists (Kahuku Farms 2020). Kahuku Farms, furthermore, provides educational tours for school children as a community service.

Market synergies recognizes that tourists can provide an additional customer base for local events or products. The Kapiolani Community College (KCC) Farmers' Market offers locally grown and produced products direct from farmers and local businesses for residents to purchase. The KCC Farmers' Market also has become a popular tourist attraction. This is similar to the San Francisco Ferry Plaza Farmers' Market where some of the city's best chefs and well-known farmers attract both residents and tourists. Local restaurants, food trucks, and other types of eateries serving primarily residents have been made popular through shows on the Food Network cable channel and now attract tourists who otherwise would not have known about the establishments.

Marketing synergies are ways to use tourism to create awareness of an area's special attributes, products, and services. Through social media, the tourists themselves become a way to promote the special products and services of an area as they post pictures and videos of their trips. The use of local products/services by tourist establishments such as airlines, hotels and restaurants, and the inclusion of the local products/services in their promotional activities is another example of marketing synergy. Hawaiian Airlines features a Chef Series for first-class meals on its flights. It uses local chefs to design special meals reflecting the culture and products of Hawaii. The airline's new uniforms were introduced in 2017. Hilo–based design firm Sig Zane Kaiao created the design for the uniforms in collaboration with employees and Affinity Apparel to encompass cultural traditions of Hawaii and the theme of employees working together to reach one's common destination (Hawaiian Airlines 2016). The airline's website includes videos on "How to Cook Like a Local" which features recipes by local chefs using local products to cook local dishes (Hawaiian Airlines 2020). With the Internet, numerous opportunities are possible to create awareness of an area's uniqueness by featuring its special attributes, local products, and services on tourism websites.

In addition to the above synergies, there are strategic actions that would produce positive outcomes under any scenario. Examples of these types of actions would include but are not limited to:

- Preserving the native Hawaiian culture and traditions.
- Managing critical environmental resources.
- Resolving conflicting needs of residents and visitors.
- Developing programs to improve the quality of life for residents.
- Developing programs to use tourism as a contributor to the sustainability unique to each island.

Each of the Hawaiian Islands differ not only in the types of visitors, but also in the economic, social, and environmental factors that affect their respective sustainability. Instead of a State-wide, one size fits all approach, programs unique to the needs of each island should be developed. Each island has different comparative advantages and limitations. The residents of each island should be allowed to prioritize the actions to be taken to improve their respective situations. Sustainability is a continuum that changes to meet new needs and not an end in itself. As more information becomes available over time, it will be possible to forecast a range of potential outcomes to improve the situation of each island. Decentralizing the process for developing strategies unique to each island also should include how each island interrelates with each other and the world. Comparative advantages of one island could be used to offset limitations of another island for the mutual benefit of both.

Hawaii has the professional expertise to take a leadership position in developing strategies to use tourism as a means to enhance the sustainability of each island. The previously mentioned planning and design companies located in Hawaii, specialists at the University of Hawaii, as well as other organizations, have the expertise to use tourism as one of the ways to enhance the sustainability of each island. Billionaire, Larry Ellison, already has plans to develop the island of Lanai as a sustainable community (Pulama Lanai 2020). Ellison owns 97 percent of the island and his company, Pulama Lanai, has been working on developing programs that serve both residents and guests to promote preservation, progress, and sustainability on the island. HTA's current efforts to develop plans to regenerate tourism for each island is a major step in the right direction but does not go far enough in decentralizing the funds and responsibility for the management and marketing of tourism to each island.

Epilogue

As one looks back at the history of Hawaii's tourism, the focus on economic development outweighed other considerations in spite of the fact that the 1957 report on *The Role of Government in the Development of Hawaii's Visitor Industry* stated:

"The ultimate goal of tourist development in Hawaii is a sound growth of income, employment and government revenues. 'Sound growth' requires (a) that programs be geared to the long range permanent development of the industry, and (b) that they do not sacrifice community and cultural values basic to the welfare of the people of Hawaii" (The Governor's Advisory Committee on the Tourist Industry 1957).

Moving forward will require a balanced approach to use tourism to meet the economic, social, and environmental sustainability of the State. Instead of Pinkham's Venice of the Pacific, the future can bring the restoration of Hawaii towards Mark Twain's description of the Hawaiian Islands as "*the loveliest fleet of Islands anchored in any ocean*" (Blum 2020; Twain and Clemens 1994).

Bibliography

"About the Boeing 314 Clipper Flying Boat." 2016. Foynes Flying Boat & Maritime Museum. October 30, 2016. https://www.flyingboatmuseum.com/boeing-314-clipper-flying-boat/.

Admin, Da Kine. 2020 "Home-Visit Molokai." Molokai Hawaii Visitor Guide. Accessed December 9, 2020. https://visitmolokai.com/wp/.

Advantage Vacation. 2020. "Marriott Vacation Club Timeshares in Hawaii | Advantage Vacation Timeshare Resales." 2020. https://advantagevacation.com/marriott-vacation-club-timeshares-in-hawaii/.

Advertiser Staff. 1996. "Hotel Values Plummet." *The Honolulu Advertiser*, March 27, 1996.

———2002. "Hilton Buying All of Waikoloa Resort Hotel | The Honolulu Advertiser | Hawaii's Newspaper." *Honolulu Advertiser*, April 24, 2002. http://the.honoluluadvertiser.com/article/2002/Apr/24/bz/bz03a.html.

Airbnb. 2016. "History of Airbnb." Airbnb. November 14, 2016. https://airbnb370.wordpress.com/history-of-airbnb/.

Airbus. 2020. "A-380 Airlines Destinations." Airbus. 2020. https://www.airbus.com/aircraft/passenger-aircraft/a380/airlines-destinations.html.

———2021. "Innovation." Airbus. 2021. https://www.airbus.com/aircraft/passenger-aircraft/a380/innovation.html.

Alexander, Arthur J. 2000. "JAPAN'S AVIATION INDUSTRY: DEREGULATION ADVANCES ON BROAD FRONT - No. 21, May 26, 2000." *Japan Economic Institute Report*, May 26, 2000. http://www.jei.org/Restricted/JEIR00/0021f.html.

Allen, Robert C. 2004. *Creating Hawaii Tourism*. Honolulu, Hawaii: Bess Press Incorporated.

American Intercontinental University. 2020. "The Four Functions of Management: What Managers Need to Know | AIU." American Intercontinental University. 2020. https://www.aiuniv.edu/degrees/business/articles/functions-of-management.

Archibald, Anna. 2016. "Tiki's Founders: Don the Beachcomber and Trader Vic." Thrillist. August 18, 2016. https://www.thrillist.com/culture/tikis-founders-don-the-beachcomber-and-trader-vic.

Atlantic City Free Public Library. 2020. "History of Atlantic City." Atlantic City Free Public Library. 2020. http://acfpl.org/component/content/article/15-heston-archives/147-atlantic-city-history-22.html.

Aviation History Online Museum. 2020. "Martin M-130 China Clipper." The Aviation History Online Museum. 2020. http://www.aviation-history.com/martin/m130.html.

Aviation Strategy. 1999. "Aviation Strategy - Japanese Deregulation: Skymark and Air Do Jolt JAL, ANA and JAS," March 1999. https://aviationstrategy.aero/newsletter/Mar-1999/6/Japanese_deregulation:_Skymark_and_Air_Do_jolt_JAL_ANA_and_JAS.

Avi-Yonah, Reuven. 2006. "The Three Goals of Taxation." *University of Michigan, Michigan Law, Scholarship Repository*, January. https://repository.law.umich.edu/articles/40.

Awani Bali. 2018. "How 5 People Helped Create the Bali of Today: The History of Tourism in Bali." Awani Bali. May 28, 2018. https://awani.com/blog/bali-tourism-history/.

Back Bay Association. 2020. "History-Boston Back Bay." Back Bay Association. 2020. https://www.bostonbackbay.com/about-back-bay/history/.

Balla, Lesley. 2019. "Can Tiki Be Done Without the Cultural Appropriation?" *Eater*, November 11, 2019. https://www.eater.com/2019/11/11/20953353/trader-vics-locations-comeback-tiki.

Bank of Hawaii Economics Division. 1980. "Hawaii 80: Annual Economic Review." Honolulu, Hawaii: Bank of Hawaii.

BBC News. 2019. "The Hong Kong Protests Explained in 100 and 500 Words," November 28, 2019, sec. China. https://www.bbc.com/news/world-asia-china-49317695.

Belt Collins Hawaii. 2020. "About – Belt Collins Hawaii." 2020. https://bchdesign.com/about/.

Biography.com. 2020. "Paul Gauguin." Biography. July 9, 2020. https://www.biography.com/artist/paul-gauguin.

Blum, John. 2020. "Mark Twain Quotes About Hawaii." Maui Vacations - Jon's Maui Info. 2020. https://www.mauihawaii.org/mark-twain-quotes-hawaii/.

Board, United States Civil Aeronautics. 1970. "Civil Aeronautics Board Reports Volume 54." Washington, D.C.: The Board.

Boberg, Kevin, and Dexter J. L. Choy. 1988. "Emerging Trends In Trans-Pacific Air Routes." *Journal of Travel Research* 26 (3): 15–23. https://doi.org/10.1177/004728758802600306.

Boeing. 2021a. "Boeing: Historical Snapshot: 747 Commercial Transport/YAL-1." 2021. https://www.boeing.com/history/products/747.page.

———2021b. "Boeing: Historical Snapshot: Model 314 Clipper Flying Boat." 2021. https://www.boeing.com/history/products/model-314-clipper.page.

Brewbaker, Paul H. 2020. "Visitor Arrivals versus Real Visitor Expenditures." Honolulu.

Brigham Young University. 2020. "History BYU." BYUH About. 2020. https://about.byuh.edu/brief-history.

Broadway Musical Home. 2020. "Broadway Musical Home - South Pacific." 2020. https://broadwaymusicalhome.com/shows/southpacific.htm.

Brogdon, William. 1953. "From Here to Eternity - Variety," July 29, 1953. https://variety.com/1953/film/reviews/from-here-to-eternity-2-1200417558/.

Brown, Jennifer. 2012. "12 Shot Dead, 58 Wounded in Aurora Movie Theater during Batman Premier." *The Denver Post*, July 20, 2012. https://www.denverpost.com/2012/07/20/12-shot-dead-58-wounded-in-aurora-movie-theater-during-batman-premier/.

Business, Economic Development & Tourism Hawaii. Department of. 1994. "Tourism Mini-Congress, July 19, 1994." In . Honolulu: Hawaii Department of Planning and Economic Development.

Butler, R. W. 1980. "THE CONCEPT OF A TOURIST AREA CYCLE OF EVOLUTION: IMPLICATIONS FOR MANAGEMENT OF RESOURCES." *The Canadian Geographer/Le Géographe Canadien* 24 (1): 5–12. https://doi.org/10.1111/j.1541-0064.1980.tb00970.x.

Caird Library. 2012. "18th Century Sailing Times between the English Channel and the Coast of America: How Long Did It Take?" Royal Museums Greenwich. November 8, 2012. https://www.rmg.co.uk/discover/behind-the-scenes/blog/18th-century-sailing-times-between-english-channel-and-coast-america.

Calgary International Airport. 2019. "WestJet Dreamliner Takes off for Maui." Calgary International Airport. Ocotber 2019. https://www.yyc.com/News/tabid/91/articleType/ArticleView/articleId/372/WestJet-Dreamliner-takes-off-for-Maui.aspx.

Callies, David L. 1984. *Regulating Paradise: Land Use Controls in Hawaii.* Honolulu: University of Hawaii Press.

Cameron, Merton K. 1933. *Tourist Expenditures in the Territory of Hawaii.* University of Hawaii. Occasional Papers; No. 17. Honolulu: University of Hawaii.

Canby, Vincent. 1966. "Screen: 'Hawaii,' Big, Long Film, Has Its Premiere: Story Is Subordinated to Island's Scenery (Published 1966)." *The New York Times*, October 11, 1966, sec. Archives. https://www.nytimes.com/1966/10/11/archives/screen-hawaii-big-long-film-has-its-premierestory-is-subordinated.html.

Cannon, Howard W. 1980. "S.1300 - 96th Congress (1979-1980): International Air Transportation Competition Act of 1979." Webpage. Congress.Gov. 1979/1980. February 15, 1980. https://www.congress.gov/bill/96th-congress/senate-bill/1300.

Center for Pacific Islands Studies. 2020. "Center for Pacific Islands Studies." 2020. https://hawaii.edu/cpis/about-the-center/mission-history/.

Center for Tourism Policy Studies, School of Travel Industry Management. 1987a. "Tourism Development in the Pacific Islands: Trends, Impacts, Options." Honolulu: School of Travel Industry Management, University of Hawaii at Manoa.

———1987b. "Tourism Development in the Republic of Kiribati: A Study and Plan." Honolulu, HI: School of Travel Industry Management, University of Hawaii at Manoa.

———1990a. "Tourism Development in French Polynesia." Honolulu, Hawaii: East-West Center, Pacific Islands Development Program.

———1990b. "Tourism Development in the Cook Islands." Honolulu, Hawaii: East-West Center, Pacific Islands Development Program.

———1994. Hawaii's Neighbor Islands - the Evolution of Master-Planned Integrated Resorts: A Study of the Development of Master-Planned Integrated Resorts on the Islands of Maui and Hawaii and the Life-Cycle Model. Honolulu, Hawaii; University of Hawaii.

———1995. "Opportunities for the Development of Health-Related Tourism in Hawaii: A Study to Assess the Opportunities for Promoting Health-Related Services to Hawaii as an Economic Development Strategy." Honolulu: University of Hawaii.

Center, National Geophysical Data. 2018. "Sulawesi, Indonesia, Earthquake and Tsunami, September 28, 2018, | NCEI." NOAA National Centers for Environmental Information. U.S. Department of Commerce. 2018. https://www.ngdc.noaa.gov/hazard/28sep2018.html.

Centers, Taubman. 2020. "Don's Treehouse / Unique Experience | Cultural Journey | International Market Place | Honolulu." 2020. https://www.shopinternationalmarketplace.com/cultural-journey/don-s-treehouse-unique-experience?lang=en.

Chan, Harris. 2020. "Sheraton Asia-Pacific Division," May 26, 2020.

Chandler, Jerome Greer. 2018. "R&R In Vietnam." *VFW Magazine*, March 2018. http://digitaledition.qwinc.com/article/R%26R+In+Vietnam/2994901/470668/article.html.

Chen, James. 2020. "Tiger Economy." Investopedia. January 30, 2020. https://www.investopedia.com/terms/t/tigereconomy.asp.

Choi, Kieran Corcoran, Sinéad Baker, David. 2020. "The FBI Has Closed Its Investigation of the Las Vegas Mass Shooting That Killed 58 People and Injured Hundreds More. Here's Exactly How the Nation's Worst Modern Gun Massacre Unfolded." Business Insider. 2020. https://www.businessinsider.com/timeline-shows-exactly-how-the-las-vegas-massacre-unfolded-2018-9.

Chon, K. S., Tsutomu Inagaki, Taiji Ōhashi. 2000. Japanese Tourists: Socio-Economic, Marketing, and Psychological Analysis. Journal of Travel & Tourism Marketing; v. 9, No. 1/2. New York: Haworth Hospitality Press.

Chong, Anson. 1963. "Economic Development of Hawaii and the Growth of Tourism before 1945." Columbia University Series, No. 8. New York: Erickson Enterprises.

Choy, Dexter J. L. 1978. "Airline Pricing of Domestic Passenger Charters." Theses for the Degree of Doctor of Philosophy (University of Hawaii at Manoa). Economics; No. 1087. University of Hawaii at Manoa.

———1982. "The Impact of Guest Mix on Hotel Staffing." *Tourism Management (1982)* 3 (2): 116–19. https://doi.org/10.1016/0261-5177(82)90007-3.

———1984a. “Forecasting Tourism Revisited.” *Tourism Management (1982)* 5 (3): 171–76. https://doi.org/10.1016/0261-5177(84)90036-0.

———1984b. “Tourism Development the Case of American Samoa.” *Annals of Tourism Research* 11 (4): 573–90. https://doi.org/10.1016/0160-7383(84)90049-5.

———1985. “Forecasting Hotel-Industry Performance.” *Tourism Management (1982)* 6 (1): 4–7. https://doi.org/10.1016/0261-5177(85)90050-0.

———1988. “Pacific Asia: The Mass Market in Travel.” *Cornell Hotel and Restaurant Administration Quarterly* 28 (4): 82–88. https://doi.org/10.1177/001088048802800420.

———1989. *Repositioning Malaysia for the 1990s.* Cahiers Du Tourisme ; Sér. B, No. 59. Aix-en-Provence: Université de droit, d'économie et des sciences, Centre des hautes études touristiques.

———1991a. “National Tourism Planning in the Philippines.” *Tourism Management (1982)* 12 (3): 245–52. https://doi.org/10.1016/0261-5177(91)90009-I.

———1991b. “Tourism Planning: The Case for ‘Market Failure.’” *Tourism Management (1982)* 12 (4): 313–30. https://doi.org/10.1016/0261-5177(91)90044-T.

———1992. “Life Cycle Models for Pacific Island Destinations.” *Journal of Travel Research* 30 (3): 26–31. https://doi.org/10.1177/004728759203000304.

———1993. “Alternative Roles of National Tourism Organizations.” *Tourism Management (1982)* 14 (5): 357–65. https://doi.org/10.1016/0261-5177(93)90004-5.

Choy, Dexter J. L., Guan Li Dong, and Zhang Wen. 1986. “Tourism in PR China: Market Trends and Changing Policies.” *Tourism Management (1982)* 7 (3): 197–201. https://doi.org/10.1016/0261-5177(86)90005-1.

Choy, Dexter J. L., and Chuck Y. Gee. 1978. “Employment Opportunities in Tourism: The Implications of Change in the Visitor Industry.” *Cornell Hotel and Restaurant*

Administration Quarterly 19 (3): 57–64. https://doi.org/10.1177/001088047801900316.

———1983. "Tourism in the PRC-Five Years after China Opens Its Gates." *Tourism Management (1982)* 4 (2): 85–93. https://doi.org/10.1016/0261-5177(83)90025-0.

Choy, Dexter J.L. 1984c. "First-Time versus Repeat Visitors to Hawaii." Hawaii Visitor Industry Profile, Monthly Publication of the Hawaii Visitors Bureau, 1984.

Choy, Dexter Jl. 1995. "The Quality of Tourism Employment." *Tourism Management (1982)* 16 (2): 129–37. https://doi.org/10.1016/0261-5177(94)00023-4.

———1998. "Changing Trends in Asia-Pacific Tourism." *Tourism Management (1982)* 19 (4): 381–82. https://doi.org/10.1016/S0261-5177(98)00030-2.

Choy, Dexter J.L. 2010. "Revitalizing A Destination- From Growth to Maturity: The Experience of Hawaii." In *2010 9th Asia Pacific Forum for Graduate Students Research in Tourism*. Ritsumeikan Asia Pacific University, Beppu, Japan.

———2011. "Differential Impacts of Visitors upon A Destination." In , 13. University of Las Vegas, Singapore Campus.

Christaller, Walter. 1964. "SOME CONSIDERATIONS OF TOURISM LOCATION IN EUROPE: THE PERIPHERAL REGIONS-UNDERDEVELOPED COUNTRIES-RECREATION AREAS." *Papers in Regional Science* 12 (1): 95–105. https://doi.org/10.1111/j.1435-5597.1964.tb01256.x.

Cigainero, Jake. 2018. "Who Are France's Yellow Vest Protesters, And What Do They Want?" NPR.Org. December 3, 2018. https://www.npr.org/2018/12/03/672862353/who-are-frances-yellow-vest-protesters-and-what-do-they-want.

Claessens, Maximilian. 2017. "Characteristics of the Product Life Cycle Stages and Marketing Implications." *Marketing-Insider*, July 3, 2017. https://marketing-insider.eu/characteristics-of-the-product-life-cycle-stages/.

Clement, Harry G. 1961. *The Future of Tourism in the Pacific and Far East*. Washington, D.C.: U.S. Government Printing Office.

Colland, Fred M. and John Child and Company. 1953. The Impact of Visitor Dollars in Hawaii. An Economic Report on the Visitor Industry in Hawaii. Honolulu: Hawaii Visitors Bureau.

Commerce, United States Congress House Interstate and Foreign. 1968. CAB Inclusive Tour Authority, Hearings Before the Subcommittee on Transportation and Aeronautics ... 90-2, on H.R. 17685, June 24, 25, 1968. Washington, D.C.: U.S. Government Printing Office.

Commerce, United States Congress Senate Committee on. 1974. Impact of Foreign Investment in the United States, Hearings Before the Subcommittee on Foreign Commerce and Tourism of ..., 93-2, December 27, 28, 1973. Washington, D.C: U.S. Government Printing Office.

Community Resources, Inc. 1989. "1988 Statewide Tourism Impact Core Survey: Summary." Honolulu, Hawaii: State of Hawaii Department of Business and Economic Development.

Cook, President Owen J. 2020. "Church College of Hawaii." 2020. https://www.churchofjesuschrist.org/study/ensign/1971/05/church-college-of-hawaii?lang=eng.

Cooper, George. 1990. *Land and Power in Hawaii: The Democratic Years*. Pbk. ed. Honolulu, Hawaii: University of Hawaii Press.

Courtney, Hugh, Jane Kirkland, and Patrick Viguerie. 1997. "Strategy under Uncertainty. (Business Forecasting)." *Harvard Business Review* 75 (6): 66–79.

Cox, Linda J., Melanie Saucier, John Cusick, Harold Richins, and Bixler McClure. 2009. "Achieving Sustainable Tourism in Hawai'i Using a Sustainability Evaluation System," 6.

Crampon, L. J. 1973. "An Inquiry into the Development of Tourism for the Visitor Industry in Hawaii." Honolulu, Hawaii.

Dayton, Kevin. 2016. "Hawaii Convention Center-Tourism Authority Still in Debt $317m for Facility, 21 Years On." *Hawaii Star Advertiser*, January 18, 2016.

DBEDT. 1999. "Annual Visitor Research Report." 2019 1999. http://dbedt.hawaii.gov/visitor/visitor-research/.

Dean, William Patrick. 2015. The ATL-98 Carvair - Section on Matson Airlines. McFarland.

Department of Business and Economic Development, Tourism Branch. 1989. "Tourism Impact Management System 1988 Annual Report." Department of Business & Economic Development.

Department of Business, Economic development, and Tourism, State of Hawaii. 2020a. "2019 State of Hawaii Data Book." DBEDT Research & Economic Analysis. September 2020. http://dbedt.hawaii.gov/economic/databook/db2019/.

———2020b. "The State of Hawaii Data Book 2019." September 2020. https://dbedt.hawaii.gov/economic/databook/db2019/.

Design You Trust. 2020. "The Golden Age of Flying: A Look Back On Air Travel In The 1950s And '60s." 2020. https://designyoutrust.com/2019/02/the-golden-age-of-flying-a-look-back-on-air-travel-in-the-1950s-and-60s/.

Diamond, Stephen F. 2008. "Private Equity and Public Good." *Dissent (New York)* 55 (1): 52–60. https://doi.org/10.1353/dss.2008.0051.

Diplomatic Security Article. 2019. "1993 World Trade Center Bombing." United States Department of State. February 21, 2019. https://www.state.gov/1993-world-trade-center-bombing/.

Disney. 2020. "Hawaiian Holiday Is Released." D23. 2020. https://d23.com/this-day/hawaiian-holiday-is-released/.

"Don Ho Biography | Don Ho." 2020 Accessed October 30, 2020. http://www.donho.com/biography.html.

Douglas Aircraft Company and Douglas Aircraft Company. Market Research Department. 1976. *The Airlines of Hawaii: Flying Boats to Fan Jets.* Long Beach, Calif: Market Research Department, Douglas Aircraft Company.

Douglas, George W. 1974. *Economic Regulation of Domestic Air Transport; Theory and Policy*. Studies in the Regulation of Economic Activity. Washington: Brookings Institution.

Ducharme, Robert. 2020. "The History of Condominiums." Seacoastonline.Com. 2020. https://www.seacoastonline.com/homes/20191017/history-of-condominiums.

East West Center. 2009. "East-West Center Origins." East-West Center | Www.Eastwestcenter.Org. January 15, 2009. https://www.eastwestcenter.org/about-ewc/origins.

Editor, APCSS. 2018. "Asia-Pacific Center for Security Studies." *Daniel K. Inouye Asia-Pacific Center for Security Studies* (blog). October 5, 2018. https://apcss.org/about/.

Editors, France Today. 2014. "Club Med: The Story Behind the Iconic French Brand." *France Today*, August 21, 2014. https://www.francetoday.com/culture/club_med_the_story_behind_the_iconic_french_brand/.

Editors, History. com. 2019. "Boston Marathon Bombing." *HISTORY*, June 7, 2019. https://www.history.com/topics/21st-century/boston-marathon-bombings.

———2020. "Arab Spring." *HISTORY*, January 17, 2020. https://www.history.com/topics/middle-east/arab-spring.

———2021. "Mutiny on the HMS Bounty." HISTORY. 2021. https://www.history.com/this-day-in-history/mutiny-on-the-hms-bounty.

Edwards, Ron. 1994. "Matson Airlines." *Airliners Magazine*, 1994.

Elvis Australia. 2005. "Paradise Hawaiian Style : Paramount 1966 | Elvis' Movies." Elvis Australia. March 8, 2005. https://movies.elvispresley.com.au/paradise-hawaiian-style.shtml.

———2014. "Blue Hawaii : Paramount 1961 | Elvis' Movies." July 22, 2014. https://movies.elvispresley.com.au/blue-hawaii.shtml.

———2020. "Girls! Girls! Girls! : Paramount 1962 | Elvis' Movies." 2020. https://movies.elvispresley.com.au/girls-girls-girls.shtml.

Encyclopedia.com. 2020. "ITT Sheraton Corporation | Encyclopedia.Com." 2020. https://www.encyclopedia.com/books/politics-and-business-magazines/itt-sheraton-corporation.

———2021. "Amfac Inc. | Encyclopedia.Com." 2021. https://www.encyclopedia.com/books/politics-and-business-magazines/amfac-inc.

Enomoto, Catherine Kekoa. 1997. "Kui Lee." *Star-Bulletin*, 1997. http://archives.starbulletin.com/97/05/15/features/story1.html.

Eta Sigma Delta, University of Hawaii at Manoa. School of Travel Industry Management, and Hawaii Visitors Bureau. 1983. *Private Industry In-Kind Contributions for Hawaii Tourism*. Honolulu, Hawaii: School of Travel Industry Management, University of Hawaii at Manoa.

Farrell, Bryan H. 1982. *Hawaii, the Legend That Sells*. Honolulu: University Press of Hawaii.

Finney, Ben R., and Karen Ann Watson. 1975. *A New Kind of Sugar: Tourism in the Pacific*. Honolulu, HI: East-West Technology and Development Institute ;, East-West Culture Learning Institute.

Fischer, John. 2019. "An Overview of the Westin Maui Resort and Spa at Kaanapali Beach." TripSavvy. June 26, 2019. https://www.tripsavvy.com/the-westin-maui-resort-spa-1533375.

———2020 "Enjoy These Motion Pictures Filmed in and Set in Hawaii." LiveAbout. Accessed November 18, 2020. https://www.liveabout.com/top-motion-pictures-filmed-in-hawaii-1532993.

Flager Museum. 2020. "Florida East Coast Railway." 2020. https://flaglermuseum.us/history/florida-east-coast-railway.

Fooks, Maureen H.N. 1997. "The Evolution of Hawaii Tour Wholesalers." Paper submitted in partial fulfillment of the requirements for TIM 325: Tourism Development in Hawaii and Asia-Pacific. School of Travel Industry Management, University of Hawaii Manoa.

Geary, George. 2016. "Inside Don The Beachcomber: The Original Tiki Bar." *Food Republic* (blog). October 24, 2016. https://www.foodrepublic.com/2016/10/24/inside-don-the-beachcomber-the-original-tiki-bar/.

Gee, Chuck Y., Boberg, Kevin B., Choy, Dexter J. L., and Makens, James C. 1990. *Professional Travel Agency Management*. Englewood Cliffs, N.J: Prentice Hall.

Gee, Chuck Y., Matt Lurie, and Pacific Asia Travel Association. 2001. *The Story of the Pacific Asia Travel Association*. [Updated ed.]. San Francisco: Pacific Asia Travel Association.

Gee, Chuck Y., Makens, James C., and Choy, Dexter J. L. 1997. *The Travel Industry*. 3rd ed. New York: J Wiley.

George, Keau. 2021. "Aloha Maids at the Hawaiian Room, Lexington Hotel, NYC," April 28, 2021.

Ghali, Moheb, and Robert D. Ebel. 1977. *Tourism and Regional Growth: An Empirical Study of the Alternative Growth Paths for Hawaii*. Studies in Applied Regional Science; v. 11. Leiden: Martinus Nijhoff Social Sciences Division.

Gomes, Andrew. 1999. "Estate Revives Big Isle Resort Master Plan." *Pacific Business News*, March 14, 1999. https://www.bizjournals.com/pacific/stories/1999/03/15/story3.html.

Gore, Wayne M. 2013. "Japan: Growing Number of Outbound Tourists | .TR." *Tourism Review News*, January 28, 2013. https://www.tourism-review.com/travel-tourism-magazine-japan-growing-number-of-outbound-tourists-article2031.

Government of Canada, Statistics Canada. 2017. "The Evolution of Canadian Tourism, 1946 to 2015." Statistics Canada. January 16, 2017. https://www150.statcan.gc.ca/n1/pub/11-630-x/11-630-x2017001-eng.htm.

Graceland. 2020. "Elvis Presley's 'Blue Hawaii.'" 2020. https://www.graceland.com/blog/posts/elvis-presleys-blue-hawaii/.

Greater Miami Convention & Visitors Bureau. 2020. "Miami History and Heritage." Greater Miami Convention & Visitors Bureau. 2020. https://www.miamiandbeaches.com/things-to-do/history-and-heritage/miami-s-history-heritage.

Grimes, Paul. 1975. "Introducing O. T. C.—A New Dimension in Low-Cost Travel (Published 1975)." *The New York Times*, December 14, 1975, sec. Archives. https://www.nytimes.com/1975/12/14/archives/introducing-otca-new-dimension-in-lowcost-travel-what-exactly-is-an.html.

Grosscup, Luann. 2001. "The Wild Frontiers Supplemental Carriers Boldly Went Where No Scheduled Airliner Would Go." *Chicago Tribune*, November 18, 2001. https://www.chicagotribune.com/news/ct-xpm-2001-11-18-0111180676-story.html.

Hale Koa Hotel. 2020. "History-Hale Koa Hotel." Hale Koa History. 2020. https://www.halekoa.com/History.

Hall, Colin Michael, and Stephen Page. 1996. *Tourism in the Pacific: Issues and Cases*. 1st ed. Tourism and Hospitality Management Series. London ; International Thomson Business Press.

Harvard Law Review. 1963. "CAB Regulation of Supplemental Air Carriers." *Harvard Law Review* 76 (7): 1450–71. https://doi.org/10.2307/1338420.

Hawaii Aviation. 2015a. "1920-1929 Chronology of Aviation in Hawaii." March 24, 2015. https://aviation.hawaii.gov/events/chronology/1920-1929/.

———2015b. "1950-1959 Chronology of Aviation in Hawaii." March 24, 2015. https://aviation.hawaii.gov/events/chronology/1950-1959/.

———2015c. "1960-1969 Chronology of Aviation in Hawaii." March 24, 2015. https://aviation.hawaii.gov/events/chronology/1960-1969/.

———2015d. "1970-1979-Chronology of Aviation in Hawaii." March 24, 2015. https://aviation.hawaii.gov/events/chronology/1970-1979/.

———2015e. "1980-1989 Chronology of Aviation in Hawaii." March 24, 2015. https://aviation.hawaii.gov/events/chronology/1980-1989/.

———2015f. "1990-1999 Chronology of Aviation in Hawaii." March 24, 2015. https://aviation.hawaii.gov/events/chronology/1990-1999/.

———2015g. "2000-2009 Chronology of Aviation in Hawaii." March 24, 2015. https://aviation.hawaii.gov/events/chronology/2000-2009-2/.

———2017. "2010-2019 Chronology of Aviation in Hawaii." October 13, 2017. https://aviation.hawaii.gov/events/chronology/2010-2019/.

———2020 "Hawaii Aviation." Accessed October 30, 2020. https://aviation.hawaii.gov.

Hawaii Business. 1977a. "A Shift to the Neighbor Islands?" *Hawaii Business*, 1977.

———1977b. "Businessman of the Year- Chris Hemmeter." *Hawaii Business*, 1977.

———1977c. "Hyatt VP Joe Kordsmeier, on the Differences of Operating in Hawaii." *Hawaii Business*, 1977.

———1977d. "Too Many Stores in Waikiki?" *Hawaii Business*, 1977.

Hawaii Department of Business & Economic Development, Tourism Branch. Tourism Branch. 1989. "A Report on Cultural Tourism." Honolulu: Dept. of Business and Economic Development.

Hawaii. Department of Business, Economic Development & Tourism. 2003. *Progress on the Study Planning for Sustainable Tourism in Hawaii: A Study on the Carrying Capacity for Tourism*. Honolulu, Hawaii: Department of Business, Economic Development & Tourism.

———2006. *Planning for Sustainable Tourism*. Honolulu, Hawaii: DBEDT, State of Hawaii.

Hawaii. Department of Planning and Economic Development. 1979. State Tourism Plan: A State Functional Plan Prepared in Accordance with Chapter 226, Hawaii Revised Statutes 1979. Honolulu: The Department.

———1980. State Tourism Plan: A State Functional Plan and Related Technical Reference Document Prepared in Accordance with Chapter 226, Hawaii Revised Statutes 1980. Honolulu: The Department.

———1981. State Tourism Plan: A State Functional Plan Prepared in Accordance with Chapter 226, Hawaii Revised Statutes. Honolulu, Hawaii: The Dept.

———1982. State Tourism Plan: A State Functional Plan Prepared in Accordance with Chapter 226, Hawaii Revised Statutes 1982. Honolulu: The Department.

———1984. State Tourism Functional Plan: A State Functional Plan Prepared in Accordance with Chapter 226, Hawaii Revised Statutes, and Adopted by the Twelfth State Legislature on April 19, 1984, by House Concurrent Resolution No. 26, as Amended. Honolulu: The Department.

———1985. Proceedings, Governor's Tourism Congress, December 10 and 11, 1984, Honolulu, Hawaii. Honolulu: Dept. of Planning & Economic Development, State of Hawaii.

———1988. "Concepts, Analysis, Goals & Activities to Implement DBED's Strategic Plan, Tourism." Honolulu: DBED.

Hawaii. Department of Planning and Economic Development. Research and Economic Analysis Division. 1983. *The Economic Impact of Tourism in Hawaii: 1970 to 1980.* Hawaii Economic Research Reports. Honolulu, Hawaii: The Department of Planning.

Hawaii. Dept. of Planning and Econ. Development. 1972. *Hawaii Tourism Impact Plan:* Honolulu: Hawaii Department of Planning and Economic Development.

Hawaii History.org. 2020. "Kodak Hula Show - Hawaii History - 1937." Hawaii History.Org Hula and Tourism. 2020. http://www.hawaiihistory.org/index.cfm?fuseaction=ig.page&PageID=493.

———2020 "Cultural Renaissance - Hawaii History - Hula." Accessed October 30, 2020. http://www.hawaiihistory.org/index.cfm?fuseaction=ig.page&PageID=440.

Hawaii Hotel Association. 1990. Hawaiʻi Ka ʻoihana Hōkele: The History of Hawaiʻi's Hotel Industry, 1840s-1990. Vol. I and II. Honolulu: Trade PubCo.

Hawaii. Office of Tourism. 1978a. *Findings and Recommendations of the State Tourism Study.* Honolulu: Dept. of Planning and Economic Development.

———1978b. *State Tourism Study-Executive Summary.* Honolulu, Hawaii: Office of Tourism, Department of Planning and Economic Development, State of Hawaii.

Hawaii Office of Tourism. 1978. *State Tourism Study-Public Revenue-Cost Analysis.* Honolulu: Office of Tourism, Department of Planning and Economic Development, State of Hawaii.

Hawaii Rural Development Council, and Office of Hawaiian Affairs. 2015. "Introduction to Hawaii's Land Classification and Management System." Revised Edition 2015. Honolulu, Hawaii.

Hawaii State Archives. 2002. "Department of Business Economic Development and Tourism 1987-1995." Honolulu, Hawaii.

Hawaii. State Planning Office. 1960. Visitor Destination Areas in Hawaii, an Action Program for Development. Honolulu.

Hawaii Tourism Authority. 1999. "Ke Kumu: Strategic Directions for Hawaii's Visitor Industry 1999." Honolulu: Hawaii Tourism Authority.

———2001. "Ke Kumu: Strategic Directions for Hawaii's Visitor Industry 2001." Honolulu: Hawaii Tourism Authority.

———2002. "Ke Kumu: Strategic Directions for Hawaii's Visitor Industry. 2002." Honolulu, HI: Hawaii Tourism Authority.

———2005. "Hawaii Tourism Strategic Plan: 2005-2015." Honolulu, HI: Hawaii Tourism Authority.

———2016. “Hawaii Tourism Authority Five-Year Strategic Plan 2016.” Honolulu, HI.

———2019a. “2018 Annual Visitor Research Report.” Honolulu, Hawaii: Hawaii Tourism Authority.

———2019b. “Fact Sheet: Benefits of Hawaii’s Tourism Economy.”

———2020a. “Hawaii Tourism Authority Who We Are.” Hawaii Tourism Authority. 2020. http://www.hawaiitourismauthority.org/who-we-are/.

———2020b. “Hawaii Tourism Authority Strategic Plan 2020-2025.” Honolulu.

———2020c. “Historical Visitor Statistics.” Hawaii Tourism Authority. 2020. http://hawaiitourismauthority.org/research/historical-visitor-statistics/.

———2020d. “HTA Visitor Plant Inventory.” Hawaii Tourism Authority. 2020. http://hawaiitourismauthority.org/research/visitor-plant-inventory/.

———2020 “Annual Visitor Research Reports 2019.” Hawaii Tourism Authority. Accessed December 9, 2020a. http://hawaiitourismauthority.org/research/annual-visitor-research-reports/.

———2020 “HTA Evaluation & Performance Measures.” Hawaii Tourism Authority. Accessed November 4, 2020b. http://hawaiitourismauthority.org/research/evaluation-performance-measures/.

Hawaii Tourist Bureau. 1928. “Hawaii (Hawaii Tourist Bureau).” *Hawaii (Hawaii Tourist Bureau).* Honolulu, Hawaii: Hawaii Tourist Bureau.

Hawaii Visitors & Convention Bureau. 2020. “History of Hawaii Visitors & Convention Bureau.” Hawaii Visitors & Convention Bureau-History. 2020. https://www.hvcb.org/about-hvcb/history/.

Hawaii Visitors Bureau. 1958. "Research Report (Hawaii Visitors Bureau)." *Research Report (Hawaii Visitors Bureau).* Honolulu, Hawaii: The Bureau.

———1964a. "1963 Annual Program and Research Report." Honolulu, Hawaii.

———1964b. "Annual Research Report (Hawaii Visitors Bureau)." *Annual Research Report (Hawaii Visitors Bureau).* Honolulu, Hawaii: Hawaii Visitors Bureau.

———1970. "Recommended Goals for Hawaii's Visitor Industry as Developed by the Travel Industry Congress at Honolulu, January 6-7, 1970." In . Honolulu: Hawaii Visitors Bureau.

Hawaii Visitors Bureau, and Economic Development & Tourism Hawaii. Department of Business. 1993. "1993 Tourism Congress: December 14-15, 1993." Honolulu: Deptof Business, Economic Development & Tourism.

Hawaii Visitors Bureau Research Department, and Economic Development & Tourism Research & Economic Analysis Division Hawaii Department of Business. 1964. *Visitor Plant Inventory. Visitor Plant Inventory.* Honolulu, Hawaii: Hawaii Visitors Bureau.

Hawaiian Airlines. 2016. "Hawaiian Airlines Unveils New Uniforms." Hawaiian Airlines | Newsroom. 2016. https://newsroom.hawaiianairlines.com/releases/hawaiian-airlines-unveils-new-uniforms.

———2020. "How to Cook Like a Local | Hawaiian Airlines." Hawaiian Airlines Featured Chef Series. 2020. https://www.hawaiianairlines.com/our-services/in-flight-services/dining-and-drinks/featured-chef-series/how-to-cook-like-a-local.

Hawaiian Isles Coffee. 2018. "Top Ten Movie Classics Set in Hawaii." Top Ten Movie Classics Set in Hawaii. August 8, 2018. NA.

Hayes, Adam. 2019. "What Ever Happened to the Dotcom Bubble?" Investopedia. June 25, 2019. https://www.investopedia.com/terms/d/dotcom-bubble.asp.

Haywood, Jessica L. 2013. "An Analysis of the Japanese Outbound Market to Hawaii." Professional Paper submitted in partial fulfillment of the requirements for the degree of Master of Science in Travel Industry Management. School of Travel Industry Management, University of Hawaii Manoa.

Heritage Interpretation International Global Congress. 1992. "Joining Hands for Quality Tourism: Interpretation, Preservation, and the Travel Industry: Proceedings of the Heritage Interpretation International Third Global Congress, November 3-8, 1991, Honolulu, Hawaii, USA." In Sea Grant Cooperative Report; UNIHI-Seagrant-CR-05. Honolulu, HI, USA: University of Hawaii, Sea Grant Extension Service.

Hill, Tiffany. 2012. "75th Anniversary of the Hawaiian Room in NYC." *Honolulu Magazine*, August 6, 2012. https://www.honolulumagazine.com/75th-anniversary-of-the-hawaiian-room-in-nyc/.

Hilton Grand Vacations. 2020. "History of Hilton Timeshare | How Hilton Resorts All Began!" Buy A Timeshare .Com. 2020. https://www.buyatimeshare.com/hilton-timeshare-history.asp.

Hilton Hawaiian Village. 2020. "Hotel History in Honolulu, Hawaii | Hilton Hawaiian Village® Waikiki Beach Resort." Historic Hotels Worldwide. 2020. https://www.historichotels.org/us/hotels-resorts/hilton-hawaiian-village-waikiki-beach-resort/history.php.

———2020 "History of Hilton Hawaiian Village Waikiki Beach Resort." Hilton Hawaiian Village Waikiki Beach Resort. Accessed November 18, 2020. https://www.hiltonhawaiianvillage.com/about-the-resort/resort-history.

Hilton Waikoloa Village. 2020. "Hawaiian Culture Events & Hilton Resort History." 2020. https://www.hiltonwaikoloavillage.com/about-the-resort/culture-and-history.

History.com Editors. 2020. "9/11 Attacks." HISTORY. September 11, 2020. https://www.history.com/topics/21st-century/9-11-attacks.

Hitch, Thomas. 1958. "Hawaii--Island Paradise with Economic Potential." *Business Horizons* 1 (5): 85–92.

Hitch, Thomas Kemper. 1992. Islands in Transition: The Past, Present, and Future of Hawaii's Economy. Honolulu: First Hawaiian Bank.

Hoke, Ken. 2015. "ETOPS - Enhancing Safety On Long Flights." *AeroSavvy* (blog). October 7, 2015. https://aerosavvy.com/etops/.

Honolulu Magazine. 2020. "Honolulu Magazine- About Us." Honolulu Magazine. 2020. https://www.honolulumagazine.com/about-us/.

Hotel Business. 2012. "Outrigger Partners with Major Hotel Brands." *Hotel Business*, November 7, 2012. https://www.hotelbusiness.com/outrigger-partners-with-major-hotel-brands/.

Hotel Online. 2001. "Outrigger Undertaking a $300 Million Multi-Year Redevelopment to Transform the Waikiki Lewers-Kalia Area with New Retail and Hotel Projects / July 2001." Hotel Online Special Report. July 9, 2001. https://www.hotel-online.com/News/PR2001_3rd/July01_OutriggerWaikiki.html.

———2017. "Hawaii's Turtle Bay Resort Looks Likely to Be Sold for $350 Million." Hotel-Online. 2017. https://www.hotel-online.com/press_releases/release/turtle-bay-resort-looks-likely-to-be-sold-for-350m/.

"HRDC-LUTPManual_PRF6_FINAL.Pdf." 2020 Accessed November 3, 2020. http://www.oha.org/wp-content/uploads/HRDC-LUTPManual_PRF6_FINAL.pdf.

Imbriani, Charles. 2012. "Civilian Involvement in the 1990–91 Gulf War through the Civil Reserve Air Fleet." ProQuest Dissertations Publishing. http://search.proquest.com/docview/1287995595/?pq-origsite=primo.

Inskeep, Edward. 1991. *Tourism Planning: An Integrated and Sustainable Development Approach*. VNR Tourism and Commercial Recreation Series. New York: John Wiley & Sons.

International Association of Hotel General Managers. 2020 "Richard Hartman." Accessed November 2, 2020. https://hotelgms.com/page/organisation/richard-hartman.

Isotov, Sonia. 2011. "Maui Now: Hyatt Regency Maui Completes $15 Million Transformation." *Maui Now*, February 11, 2011. https://mauinow.com/2011/02/10/hyatt-regency-maui-completes-15-million-transformation/.

John Child & Company. 1957. Tourism by Islands; Analysis of the Participation of Each Island in Hawaii's Visitor Industry. Honolulu: Hawaii Visitors Bureau.

John Child and Company. 1951. "About Hawaii Visitors. A Report on the Tourist Industry of Hawaii." Honolulu.

———1960. Structure and Growth Potential of Tourism in Hawaii. Prepared for State Planning Office, State of Hawaii. Its [A Study of the Economic Potential of the Hawaiian Islands, Pt. 3]. Honolulu.

Johnston, Eric. 2009. "Japan's Bubble Economy: Lessons from When the Bubble Burst." *The Japan Times*, January 6, 2009. https://www.japantimes.co.jp/news/2009/01/06/reference/lessons-from-when-the-bubble-burst/.

Jones, Blake. 2007. "Westin 'Ohana Looks Back 15 Years after Resort's Closure | The Garden Island." *Tgi The Garden Island*, September 16, 2007. https://www.thegardenisland.com/2007/09/16/business/westin-ohana-looks-back-15-years-after-resorts-closure/.

Jordan, Evan J., Laura Lesar, and Daniel M. Spencer. 2019. "Clarifying the Interrelations of Residents' Perceived Tourism-Related Stress, Stressors, and Impacts." *Journal of Travel Research*, 004728751988828. https://doi.org/10.1177/0047287519888287.

Kahuku Farms. 2020. "Farm Cafe Tours - North Shore Oahu." Kahuku Farms. 2020. https://kahukufarms.com/.

Kay, John S. 1969. *Land Development Plan and Program for C. Brewer & Co. Ltd., 1969-1982.* Place of publication not identified: Publisher not identified.

Kent, Noel J. 1993. *Hawaii, Islands under the Influence*. Honolulu: University of Hawaii Press.

Kenton, Will. 2020. "Learn About the European Sovereign Debt Crisis." Investopedia. March 31, 2020. https://www.investopedia.com/terms/e/european-sovereign-debt-crisis.asp.

Kephart, Linda. 1985. "Check-out Time: Its Goodbye Kapalua Bay Hotel, Hello Profitability for Maui Land & Pine." *Hawaii Business*, 1985.

Keyes, Lucile. 1968. "The Transpacific Route Investigation: Historical Background and Some Major Issues." *Journal of Air Law and Commerce* 34 (1): 3.

Knox, John M. 1978. *Classification of Hawaii Residents' Attitudes toward Tourists and Tourism*. Occasional Paper - Tourism Research Project ; No. 1. Honolulu: Tourism Research Project.

KPMG Global. 2020. "Our History - KPMG Global." KPMG Our History. May 11, 2020. https://home.kpmg/xx/en/home/about/who-we-are/our-history.html.

Krischke, George. 2014. "The Iconic Ilikai Apts: Rich History & Future Ahead." *Hawaii Living Blog* (blog). November 27, 2014. https://www.honoluluhi5.com/blog/iconic-ilikai-apartment-building-rich-history-future-ahead/.

Kuykendall, Ralph S. 1961. *Hawaii: A History, from Polynesian Kingdom to American State*. Rev. ed. Englewood Cliffs, N.J: Prentice-Hall.

Lawrence, B.H. 1989. "Convention Attendance Declines, Survey Finds Fewer People Are Attending Conventions." *The Washington Post*, March 20, 1989. https://www.washingtonpost.com/archive/business/1989/03/20/convention-attendance-declines-survey-finds-fewer-people-are-attending-conventions/a78a5a82-1193-4008-a73a-4f2e49aee0f2/.

Lesar, Laura, David Weaver, and Sarah Gardiner. 2020. "From Spectrum to Multiverse: A New Perspective on the Diversity of Quality Control Tools for Sustainable Tourism Theory and

Practice." *Journal of Travel Research* 59 (3): 424–49. https://doi.org/10.1177/0047287519841715.

Li, Yun. 2019. "This Is Now the Longest US Economic Expansion in History." CNBC. July 2, 2019. https://www.cnbc.com/2019/07/02/this-is-now-the-longest-us-economic-expansion-in-history.html.

Lickorish, Leonard J. 1958. *The Travel Trade*. London: Practical Press.

Lind, Ian. 2011. "Remembering the Old Queen's Surf." I L i n d. January 12, 2011. https://www.ilind.net/2011/01/12/remembering-the-old-queens-surf/.

Liu, Juanita C. 1984. *Resident Opinion on the Effects of Tourism Development in Hawaii*. Occasional Paper (Tourism Research Publication; No. 8. Honolulu: Tourism Research Publications, School of Travel Industry Management, University of Hawaii.

Lowry, G. 1980. "Evaluating State Land Use Control: Perspectives and Hawaii Case Study." *Urban Law Annual; Journal of Urban and Contemporary Law* 18 (1): 085–127.

Lynch, Russ. 1996. "Long-Time Isle Hotelier Stays Course." *Honolulu Star-Bulletin*, November 26, 1996. http://archives.starbulletin.com/96/11/26/business/story2.html.

Macrotrends.net. 2020. "Dollar Yen Exchange Rate (USD JPY) - Historical Chart." 2020. https://www.macrotrends.net/2550/dollar-yen-exchange-rate-historical-chart.

Maffei, Alessandra. 2018. "A Brief History of Hilton Hotels." May 31, 2018. https://www.torontosom.ca/blog/a-brief-history-of-hilton-hotels.

Marriott Vacation Club. 2020 "Marriott Vacation Club Goes Big With Its First Location and Sales Gallery on the Big Island in Hawaii." Accessed November 25, 2020. https://www.marriottvacationclub.com/news-press-releases/2016/09/Marriott-Vacation-Club-Goes-Big-With-Its-

First-Location-and-Sales-Gallery-on-the-Big-Island-in-Hawaii.shtml.

Martin, Emmie. 2017. "Here's What It's like to Stay on the Lush Hawaiian Island Larry Ellison Bought for $300 Million." CNBC. November 15, 2017. https://www.cnbc.com/2017/11/14/see-lanai-the-hawaiian-island-larry-ellison-bought-for-300-million.html.

Mathematica, Inc. 1970. The Visitor Industry and Hawaii's Economy: A Cost-Benefit Analysis. Prepared for State of Hawaii Department of Planning and Economic Development. Princeton: Mathematica, Inc.

Matson. 2020. "History Matson's Contributions to Hawaii." MATSON Inc. 2020. https://www.matson.com/history.html/.

May, Kevin. 2014. "How 25 Years of the Web Inspired the Travel Revolution." The Guardian. March 12, 2014. http://www.theguardian.com/travel/2014/mar/12/how-25-years-of-the-web-inspired-travel-revolution.

McDermott, John W. 1990. *Kelleys of the Outrigger*. Honolulu, HI: ORAFA Publishing Co, Inc.

McDonnell Douglas Corporation. 1971. *Hawaii - Crossroads of the Pacific; Analysis of Hawaiian Tourism and Inter-Island Air Traffic, 1970-1975.* Its Market Research Report No. C1-809-2215. Long Beach, Calif: McDonnell Douglas Corporation.

McGough, Will. 2019. "Hawaii: 5 Things to Know Before Visiting Molokai." *Forbes*, October 21, 2019. https://www.forbes.com/sites/willmcgough/2019/10/21/hawaii-5-things-to-know-before-visiting-molokai/.

Melendy, H. Brett. 2003. "Competition for Trans-Pacific Air Routes to Hawai'i 1945-1959." http://evols.library.manoa.hawaii.edu/handle/10524/623.

Merrie Monarch Festival. 2020 "History of the Festival | Merrie Monarch." Merrie Monarch Festival. Accessed October 30, 2020. https://www.merriemonarch.com/history-of-the-festival/.

Michener, James A. 1947. *Tales of the South Pacific.* New York: Macmillan.

———1959. *Hawaii.* New York: Random House.

Miller, Marc L., and Janice Auyong. 1991. "Proceedings of the 1990 Congress on Coastal and Marine Tourism: A Symposium and Workshop on Balancing Conservation and Economic Development: Honolulu, Hawaii, USA, 25-31 May 1990." In . Newport, OR, USA: National Coastal Resources Research & Development Institute.

Minerbi, Luciano. 1988. "Alternative Forms of Tourism in the Coastal Zone: Searching for Responsible Tourism in Hawai'i." Honolulu, Hawai'i: Deptof Urban and Regional Planning, University of Hawai'i at Manoa.

Moana Surfrider. 2020 "Hotel History in Honolulu, Hawaii | Moana Surfrider, A Westin Resort & Spa | Historic Hotels of America." Historic Hotels Worldwide. Accessed October 31, 2020. https://www.historichotels.org/us/hotels-resorts/moana-surfrider-a-westin-resort-and-spa/history.php.

Modern Airliners. 2018. "Boeing 747 Specs - Modern Airliners." 2018. https://modernairliners.com/boeing-747-jumbo/boeing-747-specs/.

Mola, Roger. 2020. "Economic Regulation of Airlines." 2020. https://www.centennialofflight.net/essay/Government_Role/Econ_Reg/POL16.htm.

Moodie Report. 2012. "Japanese Outbound Travel Set for Double-Digit Surge in 2012." The Moodie Davitt Report. August 13, 2012. https://www.moodiedavittreport.com/japanese-outbound-travel-set-for-double-digit-surge-in-2012/.

Moscardo, Gianna. 2008. "Sustainable Tourism Innovation: Challenging Basic Assumptions." *Tourism and Hospitality Research* 8 (1): 4–13. https://doi.org/10.1057/thr.2008.7.

Munzenrieder, Kyle. 2015. "100 Years: The Dark and Dirty History of Miami Beach | Miami New Times." *Miami New Times*, March 26, 2015. https://www.miaminewtimes.com/news/100-years-the-dark-and-dirty-history-of-miami-beach-7552169.

Muqbil, Imtiaz. 2019. "Revealed: How Alwin Zecha and I Helped the TAT Bring the PATA HQ to Bangkok." *Travel Impact Newswire*, March 15, 2019. https://www.travel-impact-newswire.com/2019/03/revealed-how-alwin-zecha-and-i-helped-the-tat-bring-the-pata-hq-to-bangkok/.

Musgrave, Richard A. 1959. *The Theory of Public Finance-A Study in Public Economy*. New York: McGraw-Hill Book Company.

Myers, Robert R. 2020 "History of Kaanapali." Robert R. Meyers Coldwell Banker. Accessed November 18, 2020. https://mauihomesales.com/news/History_of_Kaanapali/1752.

Napier, A. Kam. 2014. "Waikiki's Ilikai Hotel and Suites Turns 50." *Honolulu Magazine*, February 4, 2014. https://www.honolulumagazine.com/waikikis-ilikai-hotel-and-suites-turns-50/pic/148387/.

National Air & Space Museum. 2020a. "Deregulation: A Watershed Event | America by Air." 2020. https://airandspace.si.edu/exhibitions/america-by-air/online/jetage/jetage08.cfm.

———2020b. "Speed and Comfort | National Air and Space Museum." Smithsonian National Air and Space Museum. 2020. https://airandspace.si.edu/exhibitions/hawaii-by-air/online/post-war-travel/speed-and-comfort.cfm.

———2020 "Competition in the Air | National Air and Space Museum." Accessed October 31, 2020a. https://airandspace.si.edu/exhibitions/hawaii-by-air/online/post-war-travel/competition-in-the-air.cfm.

———2020 "Jumbo Jets | National Air and Space Museum." Accessed October 30, 2020b. https://airandspace.si.edu/exhibitions/hawaii-by-air/online/jet-travel/jumbo-jets.cfm.

———2020 "Pan Am Spans the Pacific | National Air and Space Museum." Smithsonian National Air and Space Museum. Accessed October 30, 2020c. https://airandspace.si.edu/exhibitions/hawaii-by-air/online/pan-am-clippers/pan-am-spans-the-pacific.cfm.

———2020 "Post War Travel Fly to Hawaii | National Air and Space Museum." Smithsonian National Air and Space Museum. Accessed November 13, 2020d. https://airandspace.si.edu/exhibitions/hawaii-by-air/online/post-war-travel/.

———2020 "The New Jets | National Air and Space Museum." Smithsonian National Air and Space Museum. Accessed October 30, 2020e. https://airandspace.si.edu/exhibitions/hawaii-by-air/online/jet-travel/the-new-jets.cfm.

———2020 "War | National Air and Space Museum." Smithsonian National Air and Space Museum. Accessed October 30, 2020f. https://airandspace.si.edu/exhibitions/hawaii-by-air/online/pan-am-clippers/war.cfm.

———2020 "What Was It Like to Fly? | National Air and Space Museum." Smithsonian National Air and Space Museum. Accessed October 30, 2020g. https://airandspace.si.edu/exhibitions/hawaii-by-air/online/pan-am-clippers/what-was-it-like-to-fly.cfm.

National Hurricane Center and Central Pacific Hurricane Center. 2020. "Hurricanes in History." National Hurricane Center and Central Pacific Hurricane Center. 2020. https://www.nhc.noaa.gov/outreach/history/.

Northwest Airlines. 2020 "Timeline – Northwest Airlines History Center." Northwest Airlines History Center. Accessed November 2, 2020. https://northwestairlineshistory.org/timeline/.

O'Connell, Maureen. 2012. "Rare Photos of Hawaii's Bygone 'Boat Days' on Display at The Royal Hawaiian in Waikiki." *Hawaii Magazine*, August 9, 2012. https://www.hawaiimagazine.com/blogs/hawaii_today/2012/8/9/Hawaii_Oahu_Waikiki_Matson.

Office of the Historian, U.S. Department of State. 2020 "The Spanish American War - Milestones: 1866–1898 - Office of the Historian." Office of the Historian U.S.A. Accessed November 13, 2020. https://history.state.gov/milestones/1866-1898/spanish-american-war.

Omnitrak. 2020. "HTA Resident Sentiment Survey 2019 Highlights." Honolulu, Hawaii.

OmniTrak Group Inc. 2011. *2010 Resident Sentiment Survey*. Honolulu, Hawaii: Hawaii Tourism Authority.

Pacific Basin Development Council. 2020 "Pacific Basin Development Council." Pacific Basin Development Council. Accessed November 3, 2020. https://pacificbasindevelopment.org/reports/.

Pacific Business Center. 2020 "Pacific Business Center Program." University of Hawaii Pacific Business Program. Accessed November 3, 2020. https://www.hawaii.edu/pbcp/.

Pacific Business News. 2004. "Time-Share Developments in Hawaii, Island by Island." *Pacific Business News*, March 15, 2004. https://www.bizjournals.com/pacific/stories/2004/03/15/focus3.html.

Pacific Islands Development Program. 2020a. "Pacific Islands Development Program." Pacific Islands Development Program. 2020. https://pidp.eastwestcenter.org/.

———2020b. "Pacific Islands Tourism Professional Fellows Program." Pacific Islands Development Program. February 19, 2020. https://pidp.eastwestcenter.org/our-work/pacific-islands-tourism-professional-fellows-program/.

Paiva, Derek. 2010. "Disney Gives Its New Hawaii Resort a Name: 'Aulani.' New Photos and Video." *Hawaii Magazine*, January 20, 2010. https://doi.org/10/1/20/Disney_resort_Hawaii_gives_name_Aulani.

Pan Am Clipper Flying Boats. 2020. "Pan Am Across the Pacific." Pan Am Clipper Flying Boats. 2020. https://www.clipperflyingboats.com/transpacific-airline-service.

———2020 "Sikorsky S-40." Pan Am Clipper Flying Boats. Accessed October 30, 2020. https://www.clipperflyingboats.com/pan-am/sikorsky-s-40.

Pannell, Kerr. 1985. Report on the Market Feasibility of a Proposed Convention Center, State of Hawaii. Honolulu: Pannell, Kerr, Forster.

Park, Sun Min. 2003. "Alternative Health and Wellness Tourism in Hawaii." Honolulu, Hawaii: University of Hawaii at Manoa.

Patoski, Joseph D. 1993. *Waikiki, the Evolution of an Urban Resort: A Historical Study of Waikiki as It Compares with the Beach Resort Life-Cycle Model.* Honolulu, Hawaii: Center for Tourism Policy Studies, School of Travel Industry Management, University of Hawaii.

Penhallow-Scott, David. 2007. The Story of the Coco Palms Hotel: The Grace Buscher Guslander Years, 1953-1985. Lihue, Kauai, Hawaii: Rice Street Press.

Pettinger, Tejvan. 2019. "Definition of Public Good." Economics Help. July 28, 2019. https://www.economicshelp.org/microeconomic-essays/marketfailure/public-goods/.

Pine, B. J., and J. H. Gilmore. 1998. "Welcome to the Experience Economy." *Harvard Business Review* 76 (4): 97–105.

Pinkham, L.E. 1906. "Reclamation of the Waikiki District of the City of Honolulu, Territory of Hawaii ...Recommendations, Maps, Plans and Specifications," [Honolulu]. http://hdl.handle.net/2027/mdp.39015048785623.

PKF hotelexperts group. 2020. "History of PKF." PKF Hotelexperts Group. 2020. https://pkfhotels.com/about-us/history/.

Plog, Stanley C. 1974. "Why Destination Areas Rise and Fall in Popularity." *Cornell Hotel and Restaurant Administration Quarterly* 14 (4): 55–58. https://doi.org/10.1177/001088047401400409.

Polynesian Culture Center. 2020. "History - Polynesian Cultural Center." 2020. https://www.polynesia.com/history.

Powanga, Atupele, and Luka Powanga. 2008. "An Economic Analysis of a Timeshare Ownership." *Journal of Retail and Leisure Property* 7 (1): 69–83. https://doi.org/10.1057/palgrave.rlp.5100082.

Pratt, Stephen. 2012. "Tourism Yield of Different Market Segments: A Case Study of Hawaii." *Tourism Economics: The Business and Finance of Tourism and Recreation* 18 (2): 373–91. https://doi.org/10.5367/te.2012.0112.

Professional Academy. 2020. "Marketing Theories - The 7Ps of the Marketing Mix." 2020. https://www.professionalacademy.com/blogs-and-advice/marketing-theories---the-marketing-mix---from-4-p-s-to-7-p-s.

Pulama Lanai. 2020. "Pulama Lanai | Promoting Progress & Sustainability on Lanai." Pulama Lanai. 2020. http://pulamalanai.com/.

Rees, Robert M. 1993. "Twisted Tales of Senate Shenanigans." *Honolulu Weekly*, November 24, 1993.

Reference for Business. 2020. "MNS, Ltd. - Company Profile, Information, Business Description, History, Background Information on MNS, Ltd." Reference for Business. 2020. https://www.referenceforbusiness.com/history2/14/MNS-Ltd.html.

Regent Hotels. 2020. "Regent Legacy | About Regent | Regent Hotels & Resorts." Luxurious Hotels | Regent Hotels & Resorts. 2020. https://www.regenthotels.com/corporate/legacy.

Reinhold, Robert. 1990. "'Private' Lanai Is Private No More (Published 1990)." *The New York Times*, June 3, 1990, sec. Travel. https://www.nytimes.com/1990/06/03/travel/private-lanai-is-private-no-more.html.

"Resident-Sentiment-Board-Presentation-02-27-20. Pdf." 2020 Accessed December 9, 2020. https://hawaiitourismauthority.org/media/4268/resident-sentiment-board-presentation-02-27-20.pdf.

Retire Hilton Head .com. 2020. "Hideo Sasaki >> HHI, SC - Landscape Architect >> Sea Pines Plantation >> Hilton Head, South Carolina Plantations | Real Estate Facts | Hilton Head Island, SC | RetireHiltonHead.Com." 2020.

http://www.retirehiltonhead.com/hilton-head-sc-plantations/sea-pines/hideo-sasaki-landscape-architect.php.

Richter, Paul. 1986. "Merger to Create World's Biggest Accounting Firm: Parent Firms of Peat Marwick and KMG Main Hurdman Reach an Agreement; Would Surpass Arthur Andersen." *Los Angeles Times*, September 4, 1986. https://www.latimes.com/archives/la-xpm-1986-09-04-fi-13794-story.html.

Ritz-Carlton. 2020a. "Ritz-Carlton Residences Debuts Diamond Head Tower." The Ritz-Carlton. 2020. https://www.ritzcarlton.com/en/hotels/hawaii/waikiki/hotel-overview/press-releases/resort-debut.

———2020b. "Ritz-Carlton Residences Waikiki Celebrates First Anniversary." The Ritz-Carlton. 2020. https://www.ritzcarlton.com/en/hotels/hawaii/waikiki/hotel-overview/press-releases/celebrates-first-anniversary.

RockResorts. 2020. "RockResorts Corporate Information - RockResorts." RockResorts. 2020. http://rockresorts.com/press-room/corporate-information.asp.

Roos, Dave. 2020. "We've Had 12 Recessions Since WWII. Here's How We Got Out of Them." HISTORY. April 29, 2020. https://www.history.com/news/us-economic-recessions-timeline.

Rossetti, Jacqueline "Skylark." 2020. "Hawaii Calls." 2020. http://hawaiianmusicheritageseries.com/hawaiicalls.html.

Rossman, Peter, and Gerard Greenfield. 2006. "FINANCIALIZATION: NEW ROUTES TO PROFIT, NEW CHALLENGES FOR TRADE UNIONS." *Labour Education, the Quarterly Review of the ILO Bureau for Workers' Activities* 1/2006 (142): 10.

Rostow, W. W. 1960. *The Stages of Economic Growth: A Non-Communist Manifesto.* Cambridge [England: University Press.

Routledge. 1994. *National and Regional Tourism Planning: Methodologies and Case Studies.* A World Tourism Organization Publication. London; Routledge.

Royal Hawaiian Hotel. 2020 "History of Royal Hawaiian Hotel - Waikiki History | Royal Hawaiian Resort." The Royal Hawaiian. Accessed October 31, 2020. https://www.royal-hawaiian.com/history-overview/.

Ruel, Tim. 2003. "Honolulu Star-Bulletin Business." *PBS to Buy Waikiki Site*, September 30, 2003. http://archives.starbulletin.com/2003/09/30/business/index.html.

Russo, Jen. 2013. "Sheraton Maui Resort Celebrates 50 Years on Top of Pu'u Keka'a at Ka'anapali." Maui Time. 2013. https://mauitime.com/food-drink/maui-food-news/sheraton-maui-resort-celebrates-50-years-on-top-of-puu-kekaa-at-kaanapali/.

Sadoski, Ben, and Ivan Hou. 2012. "The Goose That Laid the Golden Time Bombs: How Hawaii's Changed Hotel Industry Threatens Our Futures." UNITE HERE, Local 5. http://unitehere5.org/wordpress/wp-content/uploads/Local-5-Whitepaper.pdf.

Sakata, Thomas S. 1977. *Statistics on Canadian Tourism and Investment in Hawaii.* International Business Series; No.6. Honolulu: Hawaii International Services Agency.

Saldivia, Gabriela, Shannon Van Sant, and Emma Bowman. 2018. "Suspect Charged With 29 Federal Counts In Pittsburgh Synagogue Massacre." *NPR.Org*, October 27, 2018. https://www.npr.org/2018/10/27/661347236/multiple-casualties-in-shooting-near-pittsburgh-synagogue.

Sanders, Heywood T. 2014. *Convention Center Follies | Heywood T. Sanders.* University of Pennsylvania Press. https://www.upenn.edu/pennpress/book/15221.html.

Santiago, J.P. 2016. "The Boeing 767 and the Birth of Twin Engine Flying Over The Atlantic – How ETOPS Happened." Avgeekery.Com. January 2, 2016. https://www.avgeekery.com/the-boeing-767-and-the-birth-of-twin-engine-flying-over-the-atlantic-how-etops-happened/.

Schaefers, Allison. 2020. "Outrigger Hotels Sold to Denver-Based KSL Capital Partners | Honolulu Star-Advertiser." *Star*

Advertiser, November 3, 2020.
https://www.staradvertiser.com/2016/11/08/business/business-breaking/outrigger-hotels-sold-to-denver-based-ksl-capital-partners/.

Scharfers, Allison. 2016. "Facility Expects First Profit Ever." *Honolulu Star Advertiser*, October 29, 2016.

Schmidt, Ken, Jamie Peirson, and Mark Lierman. 2020. "Waikiki Zoning: The Waikiki Special District (WSD) Polishing Hawaii's Jewel." 2020.
https://proceedings.esri.com/library/userconf/proc98/proceed/to750/pap703/p703.htm.

Schmitt, Robert C. 1968. *Demographic Statistics of Hawaii, 1778-1965*. Honolulu: University of Hawaii Press.

———1969. "Forecasting Tourism in Hawaii; a Paper Presented to the Hawaii Chapter, American Statistical Association on October 2, 1969." Honolulu.

———1977. *Historical Statistics of Hawaii*. Honolulu: University Press of Hawaii.

School of Travel Industry Management. 2006. *Celebrating the Past, Leading the Future: The Story of the TIM School*. Honolulu, Hawaii: University of Hawaii.

———2020 "Lyle Lowell 'Gus' Guslander." School of Travel Industry Management. Accessed October 31, 2020a.
https://tim.hawaii.edu/about-values-vision-mission-accreditation/celebrate-a-legacy-in-tourism/2007-honorees-celebrate-legacy-honorees/lyle-lowell-gus-guslander/.

———2020 "Robert W. Holden." School of Travel Industry Management. Accessed October 30, 2020b.
https://tim.hawaii.edu/about-values-vision-mission-accreditation/celebrate-a-legacy-in-tourism/2007-honorees-celebrate-legacy-honorees/robert-w-holden/.

"Section06.Pdf Table 6.04 Estimated Acreage of Land Use Districts, By Island 2018 and 2019." 2020 Accessed December 9, 2020.
https://files.hawaii.gov/dbedt/economic/databook/db2019/section06.pdf.

Services, Web. 2020. "Kohala Coast Resort | History of Mauna Kea Beach Hotel." Mauna Kea Beach Hotel. 2020. https://maunakeabeachhotel.com/overview/big-island-hawaii-resorts/.

Shiratsuka, Shigenori. 2003. "The Asset Price Bubble in Japan in the 1980s Lessons for Financial and Macroeconomic Stability." *IMES Discussion Paper Series, Bank of Japan*, IMES Discussion paper Series, , no. 2003-E-15 (December).

Sigall, Bob. 2012. "Lexington's Hawaiian Room Showcased Isles in New York." *Honolulu Star-Advertiser*, June 15, 2012. https://www.staradvertiser.com/2012/06/15/hawaii-news/rearview-mirror/lexingtons-hawaiian-room-showcased-isles-in-new-york/.

Slotnick, David. 2020. "Air France Just Retired Its Airbus A380 Superjumbo Jet, a Superjumbo Which Made Its First Flight Just 15 Years Ago. Here's How It Went from Airline Status Symbol to Reject in Just 10 Years." *Business Insider*, May 21, 2020. https://www.businessinsider.com/airbus-a380-superjumbo-history-boeing-747-emirates-2017-11.

Smyser, A. A. 1990. Hawaii as an East-West Bridge: A Survey of the Economic Value of Non-Tourist International Activities in Hawaii. Honolulu, Hawaii: East-West Center.

Staff, Investopedia. 2020. "Asian Financial Crisis Definition." *Investopedia*, March 16, 2020. https://www.investopedia.com/terms/a/asian-financial-crisis.asp.

State of Hawaii. 1991. The Hawaii State Plan: State Functional Plans, Agriculture, Conservation Lands, Energy, Historic Preservation, Recreation, Tourism, Transportation. Honolulu: State of Hawaii.

State of Hawaii Auditor, and Belt Collins Hawaii LLC. 2015. "State-County Functions Working Group Report." Honolulu, Hawaii.

State of Hawaii Land Use Commission. 2020. "History-Land Use Commission." State of Hawaii Land Use Commission. 2020. https://luc.hawaii.gov/about/history-3/.

State of Hawaii Office of Planning. 2020. "State of Hawaii, About Office of Planning." State of Hawaii Office of Planning. 2020. http://planning.hawaii.gov/about/.

SurferToday.com, Editor at. 2020. "The Extraordinary Surfing Life of Duke Kahanamoku." Surfertoday. 2020. https://www.surfertoday.com/surfing/the-extraordinary-surfing-life-of-duke-kahanamoku.

Taketa, Mari. 2017. "ABC Stores Ventures into Upscale Dining with Dukes Lane Market & Eatery." *Honolulu Magazine*, September 26, 2017. https://www.honolulumagazine.com/abc-stores-ventures-into-upscale-dining-with-dukes-lane-market-eatery/.

Taylor, Alan. 2011. "Riots in London - The Atlantic." *The Atlantic*, August 9, 2011. https://www.theatlantic.com/photo/2011/08/riots-in-london/100124/.

———2015. "The Vietnam War, Part I: Early Years and Escalation - The Atlantic." *The Atlantic*, March 30, 2015. https://www.theatlantic.com/photo/2015/03/the-vietnam-war-part-i-early-years-and-escalation/389054/.

Territorial Airwaves. 2020 "Territorial Airwaves- Hawaii Calls-Revisited." Accessed October 31, 2020. https://territorialairwaves.com/index.php?page=30&id=115.

The Cultural Landscape Foundation. 2020. "Sea Pines | The Cultural Landscape Foundation." The Cultural Landscape Foundation. 2020. https://tclf.org/landscapes/sea-pines.

The Governor's Advisory Committee on the Tourist Industry. 1957. "The Role of Government In The Development of Hawaii's Visitor Industry." Honolulu.

"The Hawaii Five-O Home Page." 2020. The Hawaii Five-O Home Page. 2020. http://www.fiveohomepage.com/.

The Kahala Hotel & Resort. 2020. "Milestones & Memories - Oahu Hotel | The Kahala Hotel & Resort." The Kahala Resort. 2020. https://www.kahalaresort.com/Our-Resort/kahala-milestones.

The Maritime Heritage Project. 2020. "RMSS Zealandia Sailings 1800s, 1900s from San Francisco to Hawaii to Australia. The Maritime Heritage Project." 2020. https://www.maritimeheritage.org/passengers/RMSS-Zealandia.html.

The Week Staff. 2020. "What Happened to the Malaysia Airlines Flight 370." The Week UK. June 16, 2020. //www.theweek.co.uk/mh370/58037/mh370-conspiracy-theories-what-happened-to-the-missing-plane.

Thielges, Kimo. 2020. "Alfred Apaka Biography." 2020. https://www.musicofaloha.net/alfred_apaka_page.html.

Travel Hawaii. 2009. "News Release: Trump Tower Waikiki Hotel Opening in Hawaii." Travel-Hawaii.Com. August 21, 2009. https://travel-hawaii.com/trump_tower_waikiki_hotel_opening_in_hawaii.html.

Triple A learning. 2020 "Merit Goods." Accessed November 3, 2020. http://www.sanandres.esc.edu.ar/secondary/economics%20packs/microeconomics_sl/page_116.htm.

Twain, Mark, and Samuel Langhorne Clemens. 1994. *Mark Twain in Hawaii: Roughing It in the Sandwich Islands, Hawaii in the 1860's*. First Thus edition. Honolulu, Hawaii: Mutual Publishing.

Twomey, Brian. 2019. "The Plaza Accord's Effects on Currency Markets." Investopedia. June 25, 2019. https://www.investopedia.com/articles/forex/09/plaza-accord.asp.

United Nations World Tourism Organization. 2020. "Global and Regional Tourism Performance | UNWTO." 2020. https://www.unwto.org/global-and-regional-tourism-performance.

United States. Civil Aeronautics Board. 1974. Before the Civil Aeronautics Board, Washington, D.C., Docket 25474, Hawaii Fares Investigation: Direct Exhibits of the State of Hawaii, County of Hawaii. Washington, D.C: Civil Aeronautics Board.

———1979. Before the Civil Aeronautics Board, Washington, D.C., Direct Testimonies and Exhibits of the State of Hawaii and the Counties of Hawaii, Maui & Kauai: Hawaii Common Fares Investigation. Washington, D.C: Civil Aeronautics Board.

University of Hawaii at Manoa. 1987. "Report to the 1988 Legislature, S.R. 62, S.D. 1, Requesting the Establishment of a Pacific Tourism Training Institute within the School of Travel Industry Management at the University of Hawaii-Manoa." Honolulu: University of Hawaii at Manoa.

———2020. "History | University of Hawaiʻi at Mānoa." University of Hawaii at Manoa. 2020. https://manoa.hawaii.edu/about/history/.

University of Hawaii at Manoa. School of Travel Industry Management and Pacific Basin Development Council. 1983. "Tourism Services Manpower Development Study of the American Pacific Islands." Honolulu, Hawaii: The Council.

UNWTO. 2008. "Glossary of Tourism Terms | UNWTO." 2008. https://www.unwto.org/glossary-tourism-terms.

———2010. *International Recommendations for Tourism Statistics 2008*. Madrid: United Nations World Tourism Organization.

———2018. "UNWTO Tourism Data Dashboard | UNWTO." UNWTO. 2018. https://www.unwto.org/unwto-tourism-dashboard.

———, ed. 2019. UNWTO Guidelines for Institutional Strengthening of Destination Management Organizations (DMOs) – Preparing DMOs for New Challenges. World Tourism Organization (UNWTO). https://doi.org/10.18111/9789284420841.

———2020. "Sustainable Development | UNWTO." UNWTO. 2020. https://www.unwto.org/sustainable-development.

U.S. Bureau of Economic Analysis. 2020. "Nominal Annual GDP Hawaii ...BEA Table SAGDP2N." 2020. https://www.bea.gov/data/gdp/gdp-state.

US Department of Commerce, National Oceanic and Atmospheric Administration. 2017. "Deepwater Horizon: Effect on Marine

Mammals and Sea Turtles." https://oceanservice.noaa.gov/news/apr17/dwh-protected-species.html.

U.S. Department of State. 2016. "Open Skies Partnerships: Expanding the Benefits of Freer Commercial Aviation." U.S. Department of State. September 16, 2016. //2009-2017.state.gov/r/pa/pl/262022.htm.

USForex Inc. 2020. "CAD to USD Yearly Average Rates & Forex History Data." OFX. 2020. https://www.ofx.com/en-us/forex-news/historical-exchange-rates/yearly-average-rates/.

Vacation Ownership.com. 2020. "Starwood Vacation Ownership." VacationOwnership.Com. 2020. https://www.vacationownership.com/resorts/starwood/.

Viglucci, Andres. 2015. "The 100-Year Story of Miami Beach." *Miami Herald*, March 21, 2015. https://www.miamiherald.com/news/local/community/miami-dade/miami-beach/article15798998.html.

Wahl, Elissia T. 2013. "Tourism Planning: The State of the Art." Professional Paper submitted in partial fulfillment of the requirements for the degree of Master of science in Travel Industry Management. School of Travel Industry Management, University of Hawaii Manoa.

Waialae Country Club. 2020 "The Clubhouse - Waialae Country Club." Waialae Country Club. Accessed October 31, 2020. https://www.waialaecc.com/web/pages/the-clubhouse.

Wailea Resort Association. 2020. "History & Culture of Wailea." Wailea Resort Association. 2020. https://wailearesortassociation.com/about-wailea-resort-association/history-culture.

Walling, Kathie. 2020. "Timeline of Lanai Island History." Hawaii for Visitors. 2020. http://www.hawaiiforvisitors.com/islands/lanai-island/about/historic-timeline.htm.

Warnken, Jan, Roslyn Russell, and Bill Faulkner. 2003. "Condominium Developments in Maturing Destinations: Potentials and Problems of Long-Term Sustainability."

Tourism Management (1982) 24 (2): 155–68. https://doi.org/10.1016/S0261-5177(02)00063-8.

Webmaster. 2020a. "Adventures In Paradise | Nostalgia Central." 2020. https://nostalgiacentral.com/television/tv-by-decade/tv-shows-1950s/adventures-paradise/.

———2020b. "Hawaiian Eye | Nostalgia Central." 2020. https://nostalgiacentral.com/television/tv-by-decade/tv-shows-1950s/hawaiian-eye/.

WestJet. 2016. "WestJet's 767s Begin Non-Stop Service to Hawaii Sunday." WestJet News Releases. January 10, 2016. http://westjet.mediaroom.com/2016-01-10-WestJets-767s-begin-non-stop-service-to-Hawaii-Sunday.

Wimberly, Allison, Tong & Goo. 2020. "Heritage-WATG." WATG. 2020. https://www.watg.com/about/heritage/.

Wimberly, Allison, Tong & Goo, WATG on. 2015. "The Waikikian." WATG. June 10, 2015. https://www.watg.com/the-waikikian/.

Woods, Ross. 2020. "A Brief Review of Bali Tourism in 2019." *Hotel Investment Strategies, LLC* (blog). February 4, 2020. http://hotelinvestmentstrategies.com/a-brief-review-of-bali-tourism-in-2019/.

World Bank. 2019. "International Tourism, Number of Arrivals - French Polynesia | Data." 2019. https://data.worldbank.org/indicator/ST.INT.ARVL?locations=PF.

World Biographical Encyclopedia. 2020. "Robert Henry Burns." Prabook. 2020. https://prabook.com/web/robert_henry.burns/268689.

World Health Organization. 2020. "WHO | SARS (Severe Acute Respiratory Syndrome)." WHO. World Health Organization. 2020. https://www.who.int/ith/diseases/sars/en/.

World Nuclear Association. 2020. "Fukushima Daiichi Accident - World Nuclear Association." https://www.world-nuclear.org/information-library/safety-and-security/safety-of-plants/fukushima-daiichi-accident.aspx.

World Vision. 2018. "2017 Hurricane Harvey: Facts, FAQs, and How to Help." World Vision. September 7, 2018. https://www.worldvision.org/disaster-relief-news-stories/2017-hurricane-harvey-facts.

Yamashita, Samuel Hideo. 2020. *Hawai'i Regional Cuisine: The Food Movement That Changed the Way Hawai'i Eats*. Honolulu, Hawaii: University of Hawaii Press. https://uhpress.hawaii.edu/title/hawaii-regional-cuisine-the-food-movement-that-changed-the-way-hawaii-eats/.

Young, Peter T. 2014. "Ho'okuleana: 'Reclamation' Projects – Early-1900s." *Ho'okuleana* (blog). April 15, 2014. http://totakeresponsibility.blogspot.com/2014/04/reclamation-projects-early-1900s.html.

Zapotosky, Matt. 2017. "Charleston Church Shooter: 'I Would like to Make It Crystal Clear, I Do Not Regret What I Did.'" *Washington Post*, January 4, 2017, sec. National Security. https://www.washingtonpost.com/world/national-security/charleston-church-shooter-i-would-like-to-make-it-crystal-clear-i-do-not-regret-what-i-did/2017/01/04/05b0061e-d1da-11e6-a783-cd3fa950f2fd_story.html.

Zook, Chris, and James Allen. 2003. "Growth Outside the Core. (Business Diversification)." *Harvard Business Review* 81 (12): 66–75

Made in United States
North Haven, CT
10 November 2026

22088882R00143